THE
Illuminated Page
TEN CENTURIES OF MANUSCRIPT PAINTING
in the British Library

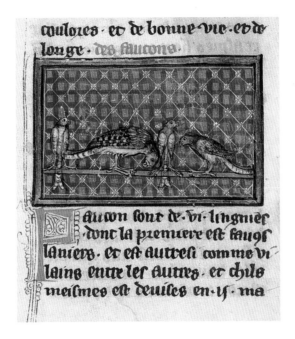

Cy commence le premier liure
de ce present volume Intitule Le
chemin de vaillace.

A glorieuse trinite
Trois personnes cognue
Pere filz et saint esprit
Qui humain lin

nage querit
Deternele dampnation

Par sa benoite passion
the dist a mon commencement
Le don de son ayde ensement
Grace pouoir sens pour retenir
Ung compte que ie vous veul fair
Dune vision merueilleuse
A comprendre moult perilleuse
Qui me aduint quant iones estoie
Et ia pres de .xx. ans auoie

THE
Illuminated Page

TEN CENTURIES OF MANUSCRIPT PAINTING

in the British Library

Janet Backhouse

THE BRITISH LIBRARY

DEDICATION

For Joyce Oxenham (formerly Parkyn née Miller)
14 December 1929 – 16 December 1993

with much love

'Far away is close at hand in images of elsewhere'

Text © 1997 Janet Backhouse

Illustrations © 1997 The British Library Board

First published 1997 by
The British Library
Great Russell Street
London WC1B 3DG

British Library Cataloguing in Publication Data
A catalogue record for this title is available from The
British Library

ISBN 0 7123 4542 6

Designed and typeset by Andrew Shoolbred
Printed in Hong Kong by South Sea International Press

Contents

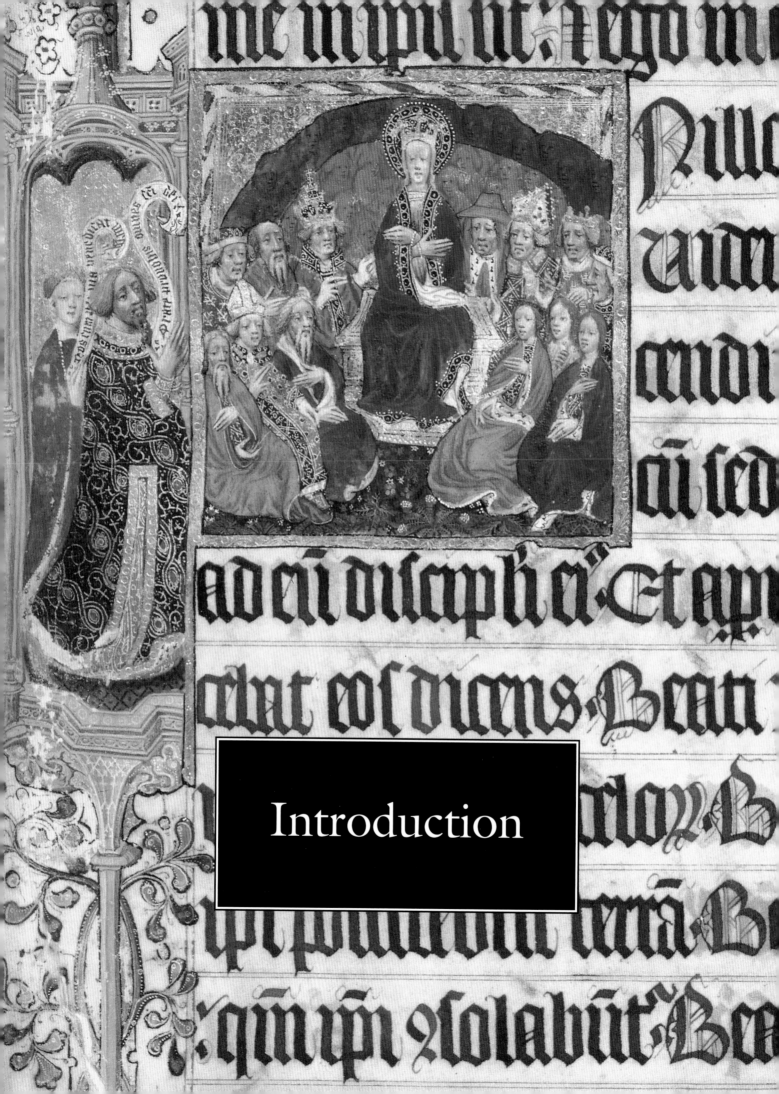

Introduction

The British Library may claim to house the largest and most comprehensive collection of western illuminated manuscripts in the world, seriously rivalled only by the Bibliothèque nationale de France in Paris and the Vatican Library in Rome. This book offers an anthology of reproductions in colour chosen from more than two hundred of them. Although these images represent only a tiny fraction of the material available in the collections, the subjects are amazingly varied. They range in date from the end of the 7th century to the middle of the 17th, in place of origin from the Anglo-Saxon kingdom of Northumbria in the north of England to the crusader kingdom of Jerusalem at the eastern extremity of the Mediterranean, and in size from the enormous bulk of the Romanesque bible from Stavelot to the pocket-sized dimensions of a tiny book of hours from Renaissance Italy. In very few cases is the miniature chosen for inclusion here the sole example of a painted page in the volume concerned. Most of the manuscripts contain dozens, if not hundreds, of images, only visible to those who have the privilege of turning their delicate pages. A high proportion of the subjects in this book have never before been reproduced in colour and many of them have never been reproduced at all.

The choice of books to be adorned with elaborate and expensive decoration varied from century to century and from patron to patron. During the earlier Middle Ages the bulk of illuminated books had religious significance. They were designed in the main for use in public worship, where the richness of their illumination could be seen as a tribute to the glory of God and at the same time a reflection of the status of the religious community or private individual responsible for ordering the work. The emphasis gradually shifted as more and more wealthy individuals began to commission books for their personal use, at first still mainly devotional in content though, as literacy increased, secular books were also selected for lavish decoration. During the later Middle Ages and Renaissance splendid books were as frequently ordered for the private library as for the private chapel. The plates here are grouped in a roughly chronological sequence (subject to the capacity of each run of pages) and each group is preceded by a brief introduction in which the historical and cultural background of the period is sketched in with a very broad brush, to help place the manuscripts in their contemporary context. Factors such as wars, marriage alliances, pilgrimages and literary developments all inevitably influenced the potential book markets of their day.

So very comprehensive are the British Library collections that most of the most significant schools of illumination in medieval Europe can be represented. The choice of subjects has of course been governed by availability. As is to be expected in a major national library, emphasis is laid upon manuscripts written and illuminated in the British Isles. The collections are especially strong in material from Anglo-Saxon England, largely because the

Detail from figure 123

Elizabethan antiquary and collector, Sir Robert Cotton (died 1631), was particularly interested in the early history and language of the country. His library, given to the nation by his descendants, became one of the foundation collections when the British Museum was established by Act of Parliament in 1753. Its supreme jewel, the Lindisfarne Gospels, seems to have been of greater significance to him and to his contemporaries for its Old English translation, added in the 10th century between the lines of the original 7th-century Latin text, than for its intricately decorated display pages. In the 12th century, however, examples of fine English work are overshadowed by magnificent specimens of book painting from Flanders and the Rhineland, a number of which come from another of the foundation collections, that of Robert Harley, 1st Earl of Oxford (died 1724), and his son, the 2nd Earl. Their librarian was encouraged to make substantial purchases from continental sources. The old Royal library, handed over to the newly-founded Museum in 1757 by George II, offers a very varied selection of manuscripts, including early medieval materials collected on behalf of Henry VIII at the time of the dissolution of the monasteries in the late 1530s. It is also particularly notable for a sequence of flamboyant library books ordered from the workshops of Flanders during the late 15th century by Edward IV (died 1483), the first English king who can be said to have followed a deliberate acquisitions policy.

Many other named collections have been acquired over the last two and a half centuries and most of them include important illuminated books. The Lansdowne (1807), King's (1823), Arundel (1831) and Stowe (1883) manuscripts are especially notable. An outstanding acquisition was the bequest in 1941 by Mrs Yates Thompson of the residue of the collection formed by her husband, Henry Yates Thompson (died 1928). His aim had been to own at any one time not more than one hundred illuminated books, representing the finest available on the market. As each new purchase was made, the least important book in the existing collection was discarded. Many smaller groups and individual treasures are to be found among the Additional manuscripts, which follow on numerically from the original collection of Sir Hans Sloane (died 1753), whose bequest inspired the setting up of the British Museum, and among the Egerton manuscripts, based on bequests of manuscripts and funds in 1829 and 1838 from successive members of the family of the Earls of Bridgwater. Of particular interest are groups from Sir John Tobin's collection (1852; MSS 18850–7), the bequests of Baron Ferdinand de Rothschild (1899; MSS 35310–24) and Alfred Henry Huth (1911; MSS 38114–26), and the library of C.W. Dyson Perrins (1958-9; MSS 49622, 49999–50005). All are represented among the plates. Major individual acquisitions during the present century have included the Luttrell Psalter (1929; figure 94), Honoré's *La Somme le Roy* (1966; figure 77) and, after the old British Museum library departments had become a part of the new British Library in 1973, the 13th-century Rutland Psalter (1983; figure 64).

Illuminated manuscripts from the Library's collections have been exhibited to the visiting public since the summer of 1851 and for the last century an entire gallery in the British Museum building has been devoted to Western illuminated books in a display often described as a national gallery of medieval painting. This material will continue to form an important element in the exhibition galleries of the British Library's new building in north London. Rapid technical advances in the field of colour printing, which have made this accessible all-colour selection from the collections feasible, have at the same time encouraged a wide use of medieval manuscript imagery in popular publishing in the form of greetings cards, calendars, diaries and birthday books. The art of the Middle Ages and Renaissance is thus increasingly familiar to a very large audience. Electronic methods of reproduction seem likely to ensure that the contents of the manuscripts will in the future become ever more widely known. It is however impossible to envisage a time at which the potential of this material will be exhausted. The sheer scale on which it survives, not only in great national collections such as that of the British Library but also in smaller public and private collections around the world, ensures that unfamiliar imagery will be emerging for the foreseeable future.

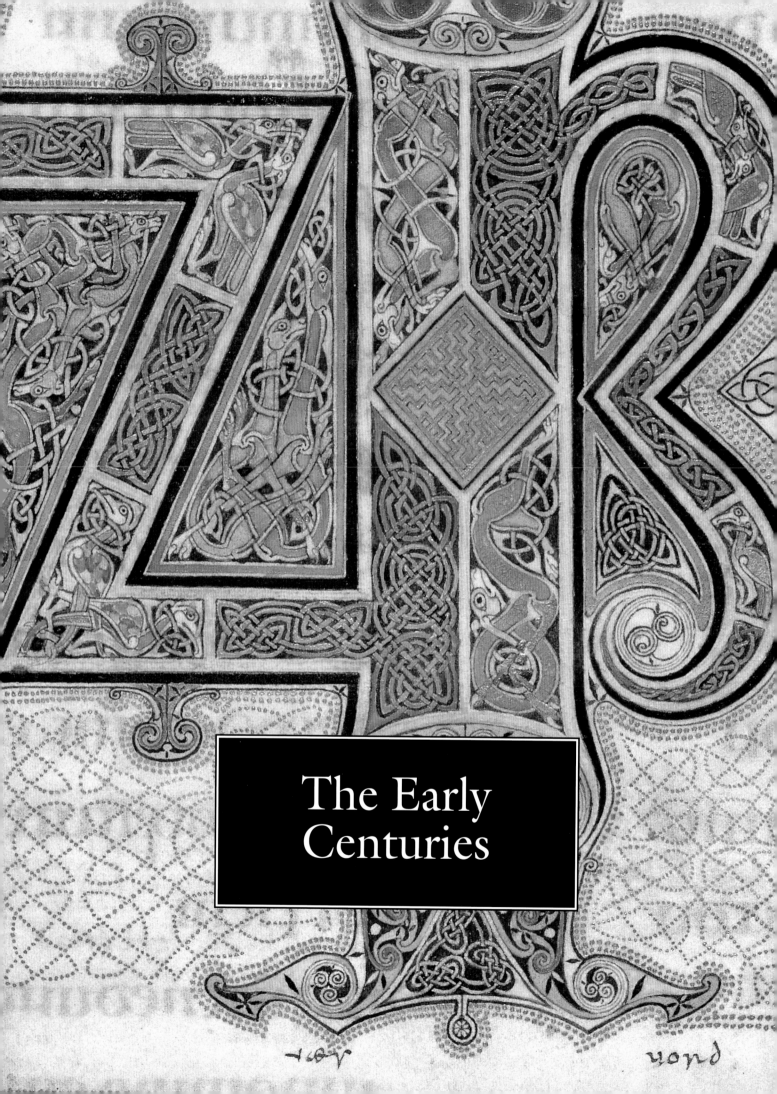

The Early
Centuries

The history of the medieval illuminated book in western Europe began with the introduction of the Christian faith into those regions which had been dominated during the 5th and 6th centuries, the aptly named Dark Ages, by the migrating Germanic peoples. Christianity is a book-based religion, its central pivot the Four Gospels chronicling the life, death and resurrection of the Son of God. Access to a copy of this text was a fundamental requirement for every priest, both as a foundation for his teaching and as a central necessity in the performance of the liturgy. Such a book would naturally be the first to inspire decoration within and without, to provide a visual focus for the devotions of the newly faithful, most of whom would for a long time have remained illiterate and mindful of their pagan roots. Copies of the gospels were thus for several centuries the target of the finest endeavours of illuminators.

Cherished with great pride as the most important single European item in the collections of the British Library, the Lindisfarne Gospels (1) is a perfect representative of this early period. In England the Anglo-Saxon invasions had completely obliterated what remained of the political and cultural framework of the Roman Empire. Christianity was introduced from two quite separate sources, by St Augustine coming directly from Rome into Kent in 597 and by St Aidan sent from the Irish monastery of Iona into Northumbria in 635. Scholarly and artistic models followed similar routes. Written and illuminated probably about 698, the Lindisfarne Gospels, which has survived for 13 centuries complete and virtually unscathed, embraces themes and motifs from Mediterranean sources alongside Celtic ornament and the lively and barbaric animal decoration native to the Germanic tribes themselves. It is however important to remember that in its own time this world-famous masterpiece would not have been the rarity that it appears today. While few copies of the gospels would have been illuminated with quite such exuberant richness, most of the major religious foundations of the period are likely to have had at least one elaborately decorated example of so vital a book. The Lindisfarne Gospels was certainly not the most ambitiously illustrated of its kind, for similar manuscripts which have survived in less perfect condition, notably those at Durham and at Lichfield, can be shown originally to have offered substantially more pictorial content when they were complete.

By the time of the making of the Lindisfarne Gospels, churchmen from England were already beginning to travel into pagan areas of continental Europe to spread the Christian message and to found bishoprics and monasteries in regions north and east of the valley of the Rhine. The influence of the well-established and distinctive insular style went with them in their books and other accessories, and played a seminal role in the early Christian arts of these areas. The 8th century saw the consolidation and expansion of the Frankish kingdom under Charlemagne (768–816), who claimed the

Detail from figure 1

crown of the Roman Empire on Christmas Day 800 in Rome itself. Passionately interested in all aspects of learning and culture and determined to emulate his Roman predecessors in the establishment of empire-wide standards, Charlemagne personally involved himself in an ambitious programme of liturgical and literary endeavour, drawing into it all the leading scholars of the day, including the Englishman Alcuin of York, whose academic background can be traced directly back to the Venerable Bede (died 735). Charlemagne's immediate successors continued his encouragement of learning and the arts. The British Library is fortunate to hold examples of two of the outstanding types of manuscript of the period, the Harley Golden Gospels from Charlemagne's court workshop at Aachen (5) and the Moutier Grandval Bible made in the scriptorium of Tours (6).

To 9th-century England the fates were less generous. In 793 the western world had been profoundly shocked and disturbed by news of the first Viking raid on the coast of Northumbria, devastating the monastery of Lindisfarne itself. The next hundred years were to be dominated by Danish invasions and the establishment of Scandinavian settlements in the north and east of the country. The monastic foundations of these areas, so integral to the initial flowering of Anglo-Saxon cultures, were effectively obliterated. Political and cultural revival began under Alfred (871–899), who is particularly remembered for his translations of earlier Latin texts into Old English in a notable early promotion of the use of a European vernacular tongue. His horizons were not confined to his own kingdom, for in his youth he had twice visited Rome and had spent time at the Carolingian court. His grandson Æthelstan (924–939) had yet wider connections, through the marriages of his half-sisters to several continental rulers including the German Emperor Otto the Great. A number of manuscripts imported into England in his time have come down to us, including the little psalter that bears his name (9).

It was not however until the reign of Edgar (959–975) that Anglo-Saxon England once again embarked upon a period of artistic achievement to equal that of the early golden age of Northumbria. With the assistance of three outstanding churchmen, all of whom were to be acknowledged as saints, Edgar initiated a programme of monastic reform based on the continental movement led by Odo of Cluny and Gerard of Brogne and directed a re-establishment of the strict observance of the rule of St Benedict. Hand in hand with this went a great revival of the arts, the first witness to which is the Winchester New Minster Charter of 966 (8). St Æthelwold of Winchester (died 984), St Dunstan of Canterbury (died 988) and St Oswald of York and Worcester (died 992) can all be associated not only with the reform of specific monastic houses but also with specific works of art. St Dunstan was furthermore himself a craftsman, known for his work in metals as well as for his skills in the production of books.

Anglo-Saxon illuminators were equally at home working in full colour and gold, and in simple line-drawing. The manuscripts they produced in the last quarter of the 10th century, generally associated with Winchester, and the first three decades of the 11th century, mostly linked with Canterbury, were outstanding in their own time and have ranked among the greatest achievements of medieval illumination ever since (10–14).

Late Anglo-Saxon England was far from being a purely insular society. Contemporary exchanges of culture are well documented and physical exchanges of scholars and craftsmen are represented here by the activities of a particularly skilful artist who can be shown to have worked on both sides of the Channel, though his style is unarguably English. He is seen (11) working in the context of a manuscript apparently written at Fleury but he can also be linked to St Bertin in northern France and to the abbey of Ramsey in Huntingdonshire, which seems to have been a particular favourite of its founder, St Oswald (who had at one time himself studied the monastic observance at Fleury). Its government was also multi-national. During the half century before the Norman Conquest one king, Cnut (1017–1035), was a Dane under whom England was for a while one element in a Scandinavian empire, and another, Edward the Confessor (1042–1066), was the son of a Norman mother, brought up and educated in exile at the court of her brother. Harold, who fell before William the Conqueror at Hastings in 1066, was the first English leader for many years to have an English upbringing.

Nor did the Conquest mark a clear-cut new beginning in the arts in either England or Normandy. A handful of manuscripts produced on both sides of the Channel were studiedly based on earlier English work (19, 20), though one unusual volume has been regarded as a tentative English excursion into a Romanesque style that did not in the event come to full fruition (18).

One outstanding early school of illumination cannot be represented with full justice from the Library's collections. Just as the late Anglo-Saxon reformers were laying the foundations for the Winchester School, their contemporaries in Ottonian Germany were commissioning a succession of outstanding manuscripts traditionally but questionably associated with the island monastery of Reichenau in Lake Constance, with Trier and with the scriptorium of Echternach, originally one of the foundations made by the Anglo-Saxon missionaries in the late 7th century. The very grandest of these books, copies of gospel texts produced at Echternach for the Emperors Otto III and Henry II, are now in the Bayerische Staatsbibliothek in Munich. Only one lesser example of the work of Echternach has made its way into the British Library (21), though two rather more provincial specimens of Ottonian manuscript painting, both from an area of southern Germany also once the target of Anglo-Saxon missionaries, are included here (22, 23).

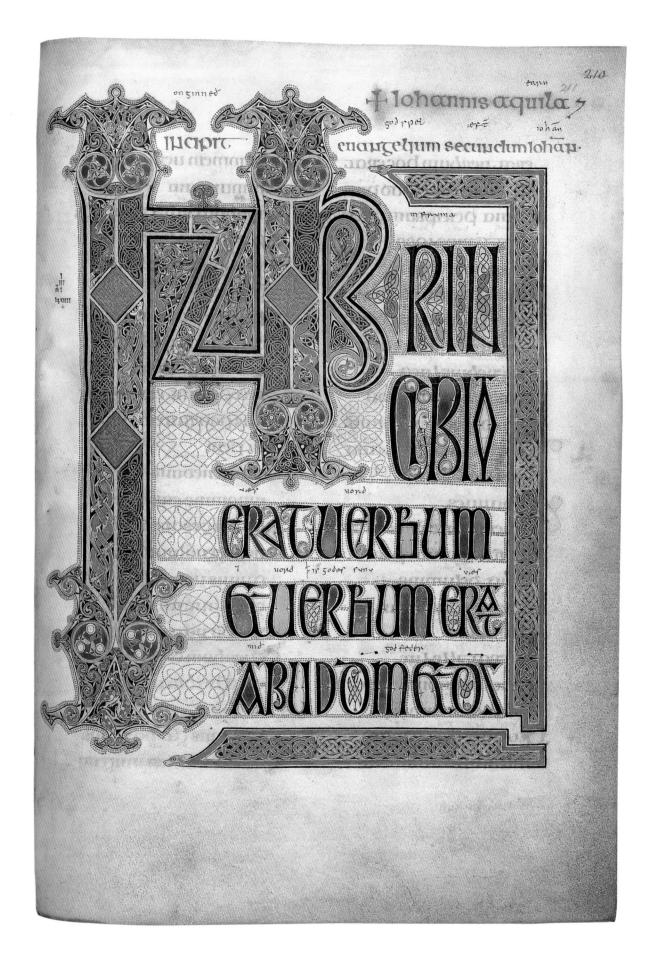

1 (opposite)

Lindisfarne Gospels

Initial page to St John's Gospel

England, Lindisfarne, *c*.698.
Latin and Old English; 340 x 240 mm, 258 fols.
Cotton MS Nero D. iv, f.211

The Lindisfarne Gospels is one of the earliest great master-pieces of European book painting. Written and illuminated by Eadfrith, monk and afterwards bishop of Lindisfarne (died 721), the book was designed to honour St Cuthbert, whose relics were raised to the altar in March 698. The original text is accompanied by an interlinear Old English translation, supplied in the 10th century by Aldred, provost of Chester-le-Street, which represents the earliest known version of the gospels in any form of the English language. Intricate patterns painted in soft bright colours fill the principal pages of this marvellous and almost perfectly preserved book. The initial page to John is the last and most complex of Eadfrith's designs.

2 (above)

Vespasian Psalter

David, traditional author of the psalms, with his musicians

England, Canterbury, second quarter of the 8th century.
Latin and Old English; 235 x 180 mm, 153 fols.
Cotton MS Vespasian A. i, f.30b

The psalms, which had formed the basis of the Jewish liturgy, became in the Christian church the foundation of both public and private prayer. This manuscript, which contains the oldest surviving copy of the so-called Roman version of the psalms (a Latin translation predating St Jerome's 4th-century revision of the Bible), was probably made at St Augustine's abbey in Canterbury. Later generations believed that it had been sent by Pope Gregory the Great to St Augustine himself. It includes an interlinear translation into Anglo-Saxon, added in the 9th century, which is the earliest known version of the psalms in English.

3 (above)

Pocket Gospels

St Luke

Ireland, second half of the 8th century.
Latin; 130 x 100 mm, 66 fols.
Additional MS 40618, f.21b

This very small copy of the four gospels was designed to
be easily portable. It would probably have been carried in a
cumdach, an ornamental satchel hung from the neck. This
picture of St Luke is the only surviving part of the original
decoration. In the 10th century the manuscript was in
England and additions were made to it by a deacon named
Edward, possibly in Canterbury.

4 (opposite)

Royal Bible

Canon tables

England, Canterbury, second quarter of the 8th century.
Latin; 470 x 345 mm, 78 fols.
Royal MS 1 E. vi, f.5

These leaves, which contain a copy of the gospels, may
originally have been part of a complete bible. In the 14th
century they were in the possession of St Augustine's Abbey
in Canterbury, where the manuscript may well have been
made. The decoration of the canon tables (a device for identi-
fying parallel passages within the four gospels) is typical of
Insular work, including ornamental motifs similar to those in
the Lindisfarne Gospels. Elsewhere in the book there are
pages written in gold and silver on purple vellum in imitation
of Late Antique work.

5 (above)

Harley Golden Gospels

St Luke; Zacharias told by an angel of the forth-coming birth of John the Baptist

Carolingian Court School, Aachen, *c*.800.
Latin; 365 x 250 mm, 208 fols.
Harley MS 2788, ff.108b–109

This is one of a series of richly illuminated gospel books produced in the court workshops of the Emperor Charlemagne. Its text is written entirely in gold and every page is decorated, the most elaborate schemes being reserved for the canon tables and the opening pages of each of the four gospels. The style of illumination which evolved for these de-luxe books drew heavily upon the influence of late classical work and also upon that of earlier English illuminators, some of whose books had been transported to the continent by missionaries working among the heathen Germanic tribes.

6 (opposite)

Moutier-Grandval Bible

The story of Adam and Eve

Carolingian Empire, Tours, *c*.840.
Latin; 510 x 375 mm, 510 fols.
Additional MS 10546, f.5b

Made at the Benedictine abbey of Tours during the second quarter of the 9th century, this is one of a series of mammoth Carolingian bibles. Approximately 20 different scribes worked on this particular book and the skins of between 200 and 300 sheep were needed for its production. Tours boasted a particularly good text of the Latin bible, revised by its abbot, the English scholar Alcuin of York (died 804), at the request of the emperor himself. The manuscript contains four full-page illustrations, much influenced by late classical models. During the Middle Ages it was owned by the monastery of Moutier-Grandval in south-west Switzerland.

7 (above)

Lothar Psalter

Portrait of the Emperor Lothar

Carolingian Empire, *c*.840–55.
Latin; 235 x 185 mm, 172 fols.
Additional MS 37768, f.4

This handsome psalter, which apparently belonged to a sister of the Emperor Lothar, is prefaced by miniatures of the emperor himself, King David, the traditional author of the psalms, and St Jerome, reviser of the Latin Vulgate text. Individual psalms are introduced by illuminated capitals and the book retains what may well be its original binding of heavy wooden boards, covered with silk and ornamented with a silver-gilt relief of a head in profile and a fine carved ivory figure of the psalmist, dating from the 12th century.

8 (opposite)

New Minster Charter

King Edgar, flanked by the Virgin and St Peter, offering the book to Christ

England, Winchester, 966.
Latin; 290 x 160 mm, 43 fols.
Cotton MS Vespasian A. viii, f.2b

The re-establishment of the New Minster at Winchester as a reformed Benedictine community was solemnly confirmed in 966 by the issue of this splendid document, presented in the name of King Edgar. Written out in the form of a book entirely in letters of gold, it was witnessed by all the leading personages of both church and state, including Bishop Æethelwold of Winchester who had undertaken the reform of this and many other monasteries. Its frontispiece is the first surviving example of the fully developed late Anglo-Saxon 'Winchester' style.

9 (above)

Æthelstan Psalter

The Ascension; initial introducing Psalm 101

Carolingian Empire, Liège, 9th century, with additions made
in England, Winchester, second quarter of the 10th century
(before 939).
Latin; 130 x 90 mm, 200 fols.
Cotton MS Galba A. xviii, ff.120b–121

This small-scale psalter originated in the neighbourhood
of Liège and was probably among manuscripts imported into
England in King Æthelstan's time. According to tradition,
Æthelstan himself owned it and gave it to the Old Minster
(cathedral) at Winchester, where it remained throughout the
Middle Ages. The miniature of the Ascension is one of a
number of additions made to the book in England and
reflects strong Mediterranean influence in its iconography.
An added calendar seems to be based on one connected with
the West Saxon court and includes obits of King Alfred and
his wife, Ealhswith.

10 (opposite)

Benedictional of St Æthelwold

The Entry into Jerusalem

England, Winchester, 970–80.
Latin; 295 x 225 mm, 119 fols.
Additional MS 49598, f. 45b

The masterpiece of the Winchester school of illumination is
this benedictional, written for St Æthelwold (died 984) by his
chaplain Godeman, a monk of the Old Minster at Winchester.
A benedictional contains special blessings to be pronounced
personally by the bishop during Mass on feast days. Each of
the principal festivals of the church year and a number of the
most important saints, including Winchester's special patron,
St Swithun, are represented among its 28 surviving miniatures. Christ's entry into Jerusalem introduces the blessing
appropriate to Palm Sunday.

ad conuexa retro celi se per loca portat.
icuti cu ceptant tibitos contingere portus
buerunt nauim magno cu pondere nautæ.
duersaq trahunt obtata ad littora pupim.
ic conuersa utetus sup acheta uertitur argo.
tq usq prora ac cæli sumu sine lumine malu
maload pupim clara cu luce uidetur
nde gubernaculu desper so lumine fulgens
lari posteriora camsuffugia clarent t candent

Coetus subariete &
piscib; gra di ens
hæb & stellas in
cauda ii obscuras.
A cauda usq ad
gippbu vi Inuen
tre vi
Sunt oms xiiii

11 (above)

Aratus of Soli: 'Phaenomena'

The constellation Cetus, the sea monster from which Perseus rescued Andromeda

France, Fleury, decorated by an English artist, late 10th century.
Latin; 295 x 210 mm, 93 fols.
Harley MS 2506, f.42 (detail)

Aratus was a Greek stoic philosopher who lived during the 3rd century BC. His 'Phaenomena', in a Latin verse translation by Cicero, was a fundamental work of reference for medieval astronomers. This copy was made at the Benedictine monastery of Fleury on the river Loire, which had close links with the monastic reform movement in late 10th-century England. Its anonymous English artist is one of the great masters of the period. His work, both tinted line drawings and fully coloured illuminations, is found in a number of manuscripts, several apparently produced in continental monasteries, which suggests that he travelled extensively on both sides of the Channel.

12 (opposite)

Harley Psalter

Illustration to Psalm 111

England, Canterbury, second and third decades of the 11th century.
Latin; 380 x 310 mm, 73 fols.
Harley MS 603, f.57b

The Harley Psalter is the earliest of three surviving medieval 'copies' of the Carolingian Utrecht Psalter, which was made at Reims about 820 and brought to England, apparently to Christ Church cathedral monastery in Canterbury, at the end of the 10th century. The Reims style exercised a strong formative influence on the development of late Anglo-Saxon book decoration and particularly on the coloured line drawing which was especially popular in England. Each psalm is preceded by an illustration in which its text is translated, sometimes almost word for word, into visual form.

& equitate
Redemptionem misit po
pulo suo. mandauit ine
ternum. testamentum

suum. scm & terribile
nomen eius
Initium sapientiae timor
dni. intellectus bonus

omnibus facientibus eā
Laudatio eius. manet in
seculum seculi

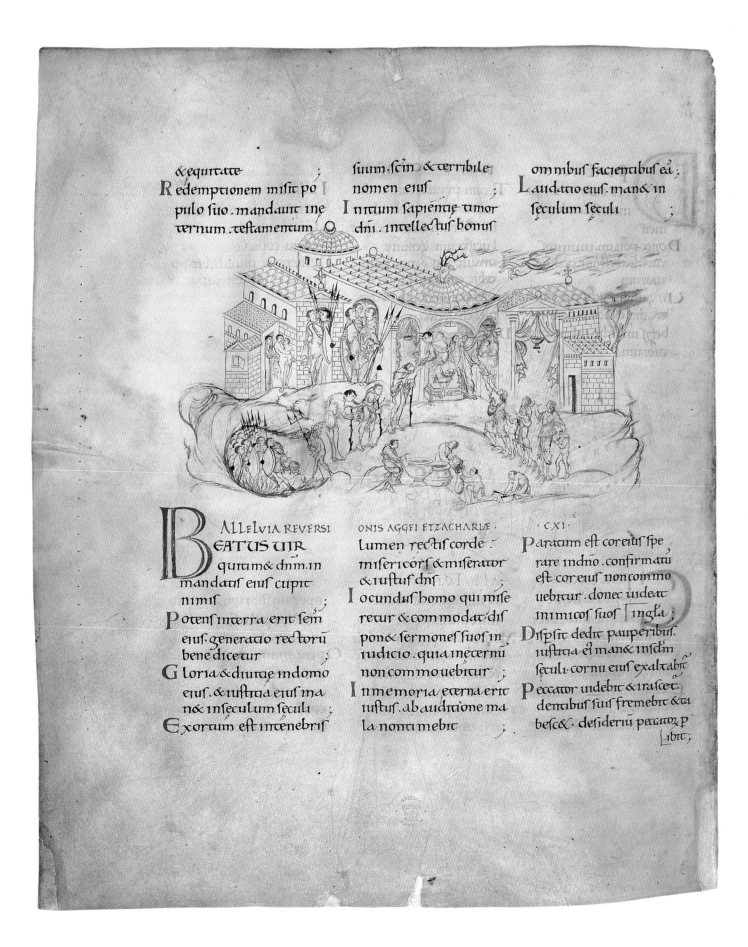

BAlleluia reversi
BEATUS UIR
qui timet dnm. in
mandatis eius cupit
nimis
Potens interra erit sem
eius. generatio rectoru
benedicetur
Gloria & diuitiae indomo
eius. & iustitia eius ma
net inseculum seculi
Exortum est intenebris

ONIS AGGEI ETZACHARIAE.
lumen rectis corde:
misericors & miserator
& iustus dns
Iocundus homo qui mise
retur & commodat dis
ponet sermones suos in
iudicio. quia ineternū
non commouebitur;
In memoria eterna erit
iustus. ab auditione ma
la non timebit

· CXI ·
Paratum est coreius spe
rare indno. confirmatū
est cor eius non commo
uebitur. donec uideat
inimicos suos singla;
Dispsit dedit pauperibus.
iustitia eī manet inscdm
seculi. cornu eius exaltabit
Peccator uidebit & irascet
dentibus suis fremebit & ta
besce& . desideriū peccatorū p
ibit;

13 (opposite)

Bury Gospels

Canon tables

England, Canterbury, early 11th century.
Latin; 265 x 200 mm, 141 fols.
Harley MS 76, f.9b

This is one of a series of magnificently illuminated copies of the gospels produced in England during the first half of the 11th century. Although they are connected by circumstantial evidence with a variety of different churches, stylistic and scribal links suggest that most of them were written to order in the scriptorium of Christ Church at Canterbury. This particular volume contains added documents relating to the monastery of Bury St Edmunds in Suffolk, including King Cnut's charter of privileges granted to the community in 1021-3.

14 (above)

Eadui Psalter

St Benedict and the monks of Christ Church, Canterbury

England, Canterbury, 1012–23.
Latin; 290 x 170 mm, 193 fols.
Arundel MS 155, f.133.

A leading member of the Christ Church scriptorium, a monk named Eadui Basan, was the scribe and probably also the illuminator of this manuscript. He has portrayed himself kneeling at the feet of St Benedict and offering him the book. This miniature offers the best surviving example of a deliberate marriage between line drawing and fully coloured painting, stressing the importance of the principal figures in the composition.

15 (above)

Prayerbook of Ælfwine of Winchester

The 'Quinity'

England, Winchester, before 1032–5.
Latin; 130 x 95 mm, 93 fols.
Cotton MS Titus D. xxvii, f.75b

This is the second part of a personal manual of devotion written for Ælfwine before he became abbot of the New Minster at Winchester some time between 1032 and 1035. A number of hands contributed to the manuscript, one of them named as a monk, Ælsinus. The compilation includes three illustrations in coloured line drawing. In this very unusual representation of the Holy Trinity, God the Father and God the Son are joined by the Virgin and Child, over whom God the Holy Spirit is hovering.

16 (opposite)

Tiberius Psalter

The Harrowing of Hell

England, Winchester, mid 11th century.
Latin and Old English; 250 x 145 mm, 129 fols.
Cotton MS Tiberius C. vi, f.14

At the beginning of this manuscript is a series of 16 coloured drawings of scenes from the lives of David and of Christ. It is the earliest surviving psalter in which such an independent series occurs, though the arrangement was to become very popular in later centuries. The Harrowing of Hell is powerfully portrayed, with an enormous figure of Christ stooping to deliver Adam and Eve and their companions from the mouth of the underworld. The Latin text of the psalms is provided with a continuous Old English gloss. This is one of the manuscripts that was quite severely damaged when the building housing the Cotton library caught fire in 1731.

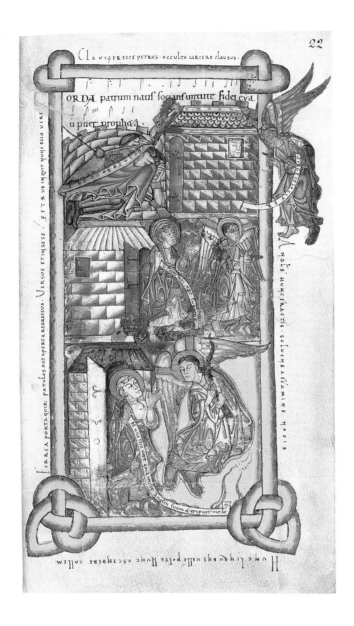

17 (opposite)

Ælfric's Anglo-Saxon Hexateuch

The story of Adam and Eve

England, Canterbury, second quarter of the 11th century.
Old English; 330 x 220 mm, 156 fols.
Cotton MS Claudius B. iv, f. 7b

Ælfric was the most distinguished scholar and the most
accomplished writer of Old English prose in the later Anglo-
Saxon period. A pupil of St Æthelwold at Winchester, he was
later a monk at Cerne and then the first abbot of Eynsham,
near Oxford. He died about 1020. During his time at Cerne
he translated substantial parts of the Old Testament into the
vernacular. This copy, which contains more than 400 illustrations, many of them unfinished, was probably made at St
Augustine's in Canterbury and may have been intended for a
secular rather than a monastic patron.

18 (above)

Troper

St Peter released from prison by an angel

England, the West Country, mid 11th century.
Latin; 195 x 100 mm, 117 fols.
Cotton MS Caligula A. xiv, f.22

The first part of this volume is a fragmentary collection of
tropes, which are musical and textual additions to the standard liturgy. It includes 11 miniatures, several of very unusual
subjects, marking particular feasts. This one, representing an
episode from the life of the Apostle Peter, introduces the
Feast of St Peter's Chains on 1 August. Stylistically it is related to miniatures in a copy of the gospels traditionally linked
with Hereford and now at Pembroke College, Cambridge.

19 (above)

Psalter

The Crucifixion; initial to Psalm 51

England, Winchester, second half of the 11th century.
Latin and Old English; 305 x 190 mm, 149 fols.
Arundel MS 60, ff.52b–53.

Two illustrations of the Crucifixion are included in this psalter. The first is in the coloured line drawing so widely favoured by Anglo-Saxon artists earlier in the century and was probably executed not long before the Norman Conquest. This, the second, though clearly influenced by earlier Winchester work, is also reminiscent of continental illumination and may be by a later and possibly foreign hand.

21 (opposite, below)

Gospels

The evangelist Mark; the Nativity

Ottonian Empire, Echternach, mid 11th century.
Latin; 255 x 190 mm, 199 fols.
Harley MS 2821, ff.67b–68

The monastery of Echternach, in modern Luxembourg, was founded in 698 by English missionaries from Northumbria. In the first half of the 11th century it developed a superb scriptorium which was particularly famed for its richly illuminated gospel books and worked under the patronage of the imperial court. This manuscript, which may have been produced for a bishop of Metz or Toul, includes miniatures of the four evangelists and scenes from the life of Christ, together with a splendid sequence of canon table arcades.

20 (right)

Préaux Gospels

The evangelist Mark

Normandy, Préaux, end of the 11th century.
Latin; 275 x 185 mm, 169 fols.
Additional MS 11850, f.61b

This flamboyant gospels, once attributed to the scriptorium of the monastery of St Ouen at Rouen, is now known to have come from the abbey of Préaux, also in Normandy. Its illuminator was clearly very much influenced by knowledge of earlier English works of the Winchester school, but his preferred range of pigments is far removed from that of his Anglo-Saxon predecessors. The figures of his evangelists look forward to the work of the following century.

22 (above)

Sacramentary

The Three Maries at the tomb of Christ; initial letter for Easter Sunday

Bavaria, Seeon, 1020–50.
Latin; 295 x 220 mm, 212 fols.
Harley MS 2908, ff. 53b–54

A sacramentary contains the texts which are said by the celebrant during Mass. The liturgical content of this handsome book links it with Augsburg and its calendar includes numerous local saints and commemorations of early bishops, including Eberhard (died 1047). It probably dates from the time of his successor, Bishop Henry II (1047-63), who was of some political importance as the guardian of the young Emperor Henry IV. Recently it has been recognised that the manuscript was written and illuminated in the scriptorium of the Benedictine monastery of Seeon.

23 (opposite)

Gospel Lectionary

The Ascension

Swabia, possibly Hirsau, *c*.1100.
Latin; 260 x 185 mm, 51 fols.
Egerton MS 809, f.33b

Towards the end of the 11th century the south German monastery of Hirsau in Swabia became a prominent centre of religious life, introducing the customs of Cluny and influencing the reform of other houses. It was possibly the source of this handsome volume of gospel readings for use at Mass, the miniatures in which are descended from Ottonian work of the earlier part of the century. The manuscript has also been associated with the abbey of St Maximin at Trier.

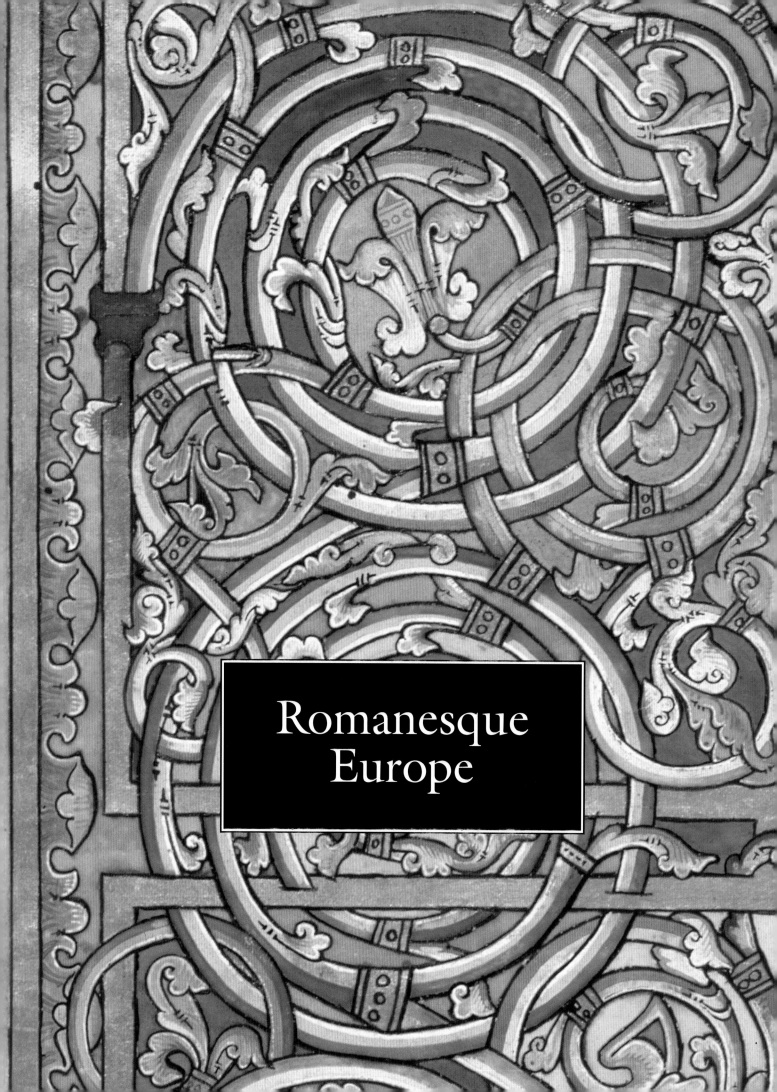

Romanesque
Europe

The term 'Romanesque' is particularly associated with the architectural style of the late 11th and 12th centuries, a period which produced such masterpieces of church building as the cathedrals of Durham and Ely and the abbey churches of Vézelay and St Denis. Manuscript work of the same period is dominated by the production of large-scale complete bibles. These were not unique to the time. One of the most famous surviving books from early Anglo-Saxon England, the Codex Amiatinus now in the Laurentian Library in Florence, is known to have been one of three large single-volume bibles, or 'pandects', produced in the community of Wearmouth-Jarrow at the order of Abbot Ceolfrid (died 716). Two were intended to be placed in the churches of the sister monasteries, where they would be available for reference. The third, Amiatinus itself, was designed as a gift for the pope, to whom Ceolfrid planned to present it at the end of his last journey to Rome, never completed. An 8th-century gospels from Canterbury (4) may also have been part of a complete bible. Within the 9th-century Carolingian Empire Tours is particularly associated with the production of massive illuminated bibles (6) which seem to have been destined for the use of communities in various parts of the realm.

The great Romanesque bibles, usually divided into two or three volumes, were produced throughout Europe. The grandest of the surviving English examples, from Bury St Edmunds, from St Augustine's at Canterbury and from Winchester cathedral priory, are now to be found at Corpus Christi College in Cambridge, in Lambeth Palace library and at Winchester itself. The British Library collections are unexpectedly rich in examples from communities in the valleys of the Rhine and Maas (35, 36, 39, 41), plus a single distinctive example from the south of France (27). These great bibles are almost invariably monastic and, exemplifying the wealth and status of the houses which owned and often apparently produced them, would have been used not just as works of reference but particularly for reading aloud from a lectern in chapter house or refectory. The Arnstein bible (41) is accompanied by a similarly enormous three-volume set of lives of the saints (42) which, though decorated with less richness than the bible, was intended for similar use.

The books reflect a considerable expansion in monastic life during the 12th century. New orders were appearing. The Cistercians, established in 1098, were particularly successful though the well-known aversion of their subsequent superior, St Bernard of Clairvaux (1115–1153), to potentially distracting forms of decoration limited their contribution to the history of the book arts. However, the Premonstratensians, founded in 1120, were especially active in manuscript production. The valleys of the Rhine and Maas, from which so many of these bibles originate, were major trading routes, linking many of the most important centres in Germany and the Low Countries, as indeed they do to this day. The same area was also famed for the

Detail from figure 36

production of goldsmiths' work and enamelling, most of which was destined to adorn the great churches of the time.

The two earliest English manuscripts in this Romanesque group still look back very obviously to their pre-Conquest roots, relying heavily upon the technique of coloured line-drawing so much in favour with their Anglo-Saxon forebears for their effect (26, 28). The 12th century was well advanced before English book painters produced a successor – or at least a surviving successor – to the pioneering full-page sequences of scenes from the lives of Christ and of King David found in the mid-11th-century Tiberius Psalter (16). The St Albans Psalter, now in Hildesheim, is the earliest contender. Made about 1120 for the use of the anchoress Christina of Markyate at the order of the abbot of St Albans, it contains a series of some 40 full-page miniatures. The less ambitiously illustrated but equally elegant Shaftesbury Psalter (31), also made for a woman owner, dates from around the end of the reign of Henry I (1100–1135).

A third illustrated psalter (37), almost as rich in content as the St Albans book and apparently produced at Winchester, seems to have belonged to Bishop Henry of Blois (died 1171), a grandson of William the Conqueror and half-brother of King Stephen. He was much concerned in the disastrous civil war between Stephen and his cousin Matilda during the middle years of the century. Matilda, widow of the German Emperor Henry V, was Henry I's only surviving direct heir while Stephen, son of Henry I's sister, was the nearest male claimant to the crown. Henry of Blois personifies many of the tensions existing between church and state during the 12th century. For all that he was a professed monk, brought up from his earliest youth in the strict traditions of the abbey of Cluny, he was of royal blood and, as bishop of Winchester and papal legate to England, a great secular magnate as well as a spiritual lord. Although at first he supported his brother, he transferred his allegiance to Matilda when Stephen attempted to subject churchmen to secular jurisdiction.

A more dramatic demonstration of these tensions was to come in the succeeding reign, in events that have remained famous down the centuries. Matilda lived until 1164, but it was the son of her second marriage to Geoffrey of Anjou who succeeded to the throne as Henry II when Stephen died in 1154. He has achieved everlasting notoriety for his part in the death of St Thomas Becket, Archbishop of Canterbury, cut down in his own cathedral on 29 December 1170 by four knights who believed themselves to be acting in accordance with the wishes of the king, frustrated in his desire to see the interests of the church subjected to the will of the crown. Under Henry II England had become part of a substantial European state which included much of western France, inherited from his father, or acquired through his marriage to Eleanor of Aquitaine. His children had contracted political marriages which linked him with Saxony, northern Spain and Sicily. News of Becket's assassination spread very rapidly through all these countries and beyond, following trade routes, pilgrim roads, and the march of the crusaders to the Holy Land. Within a few years the murdered archbishop had been depicted as a martyr in the mosaics of the cathedral of Monreale and in the splendid gospels of Henry the Lion of Saxony, now in Wolfenbüttel. He was canonised in 1173 and his shrine in Canterbury cathedral became the focus of one of the most popular pilgrimages in Europe.

The four knights directly responsible for Becket's death were sentenced by the pope to spend 14 years fighting in the Holy Land. Church and state were at least superficially at one in their support for the crusades, first preached by Pope Urban II at the Council of Clermont in 1095 in response to a plea from the Byzantine emperor for aid against the Moslems. Ostensibly the crusades were religious wars, undertaken by pious Christians in return for spiritual benefits. On a more realistic plane they offered opportunities for material gain and, for their leaders, scope for expansion into new territories. The Latin Kingdom of Jerusalem was established in 1099 as a result of the First Crusade and swiftly developed its own customs and institutions, including a very fine scriptorium at the church of the Holy Sepulchre. The British Library is privileged to hold the most beautiful of the surviving books from Crusader Jerusalem, the illuminated psalter of Queen Melisende (30), apparently made during the lifetime of her husband, Fulk of Anjou, who was by his previous marriage the grandfather of Henry II of England.

The crusades were an international concern and throughout their history they reflected the politics of contemporary Europe, none more so than the Third Crusade (1189–1192), which was marred by the quarrels of Richard I, 'the Lionheart', of England and Philip Augustus of France. It is however the story of Richard's struggle against the Turkish leader, Saladin, and of their great admiration for each other's qualities, that has captured the imagination of subsequent generations.

Although most of the illuminated books produced during the 12th century have some connection with religious observances, usually of a public rather than a private nature, there are a few exceptions. The bestiary (40) or the medical and herbal collections (38, 45), though looking back to the scientific books of late Antiquity, do reflect a widening of horizons for practitioners of the book arts. The lively drawing of St Martin and his hunting companions (48), firmly placed in its own times and closely related to the goldsmiths' work of the late 12th century, provides a wonderful demonstration of creativity at the end of the period.

MACROBIVS AMBROSIVS. ſ Cuſtachi fili ei.

24 (opposite)

Stavelot Bible

Christ in Majesty

Mosan region, Stavelot, 1093–7.
Latin; 580 x 390 mm, 240 fols.
Additional MS 28107, f.136.

Each of the two volumes of this enormous bible contains a colophon stating that it was written, illuminated and bound by two monks, Goderannus and Ernesto, who completed it in 1097 after four years' work. They were members of the Benedictine community of Stavelot in modern Belgium, about 30 miles south-west of Aachen. This spectacular painting of Christ in Majesty, which prefaces the New Testament, was contributed by a third artist who was probably used to working on a monumental scale.

25 (above)

Macrobius: 'Commentarium in Somnium Scipionis'

The author presenting the book to his son

Italy, c.1100.
Latin; 230 x 150 mm, 77 fols.
Egerton MS 2976, f.8b

In this rare Italian line drawing, Macrobius, a Roman grammarian and philosopher who flourished at the beginning of the 5th century AD, is shown presenting his commentary on the 'Somnium Scipionis' to his son Eustachius. Scipio's work describes the life of the good after death and his views on the constitution of the universe allowed Macrobius to write about the astronomical theories of his own age.

26

Lives of the Saints (Passional)

The martyrdom of St Demetrius

England, Canterbury, c.1100–20.
Latin; 335 x 220 mm, 229 fols.
Arundel MS 91, f.107 (detail)

Demetrius, a native of Thessalonica, was stabbed to death by order of Galerius Maximianus, a contemporary of the infamous Emperor Diocletian. His fate is depicted in an historiated initial at the beginning of his Life in this manuscript made in the Benedictine abbey of St Augustine at Canterbury. Although it was produced approximately four decades after the Norman Conquest, the decorative style of the book still depends very largely upon the coloured line-drawing tradition of Anglo-Saxon England.

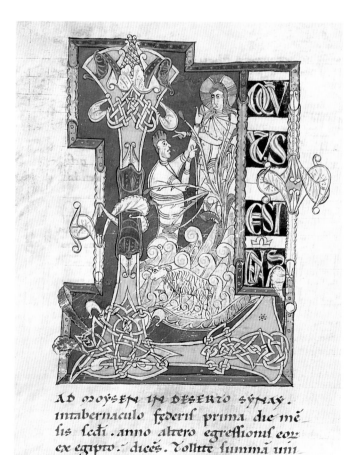

27

Montpellier Bible

Moses and the Burning Bush

France, Languedoc, first quarter of the 12th century.
Latin; 510 x 370 mm, 301 fols.
Harley MS 4772, f.61b (detail)

Two artists were responsible for the lively, even somewhat barbaric, decorated initials in this little-known two-volume bible, which was made in southern France. Influence from both Italy and Catalonia has been suggested. The original home of the bible has not been identified. Early in the 17th century it belonged to the Capucines in Montpellier.

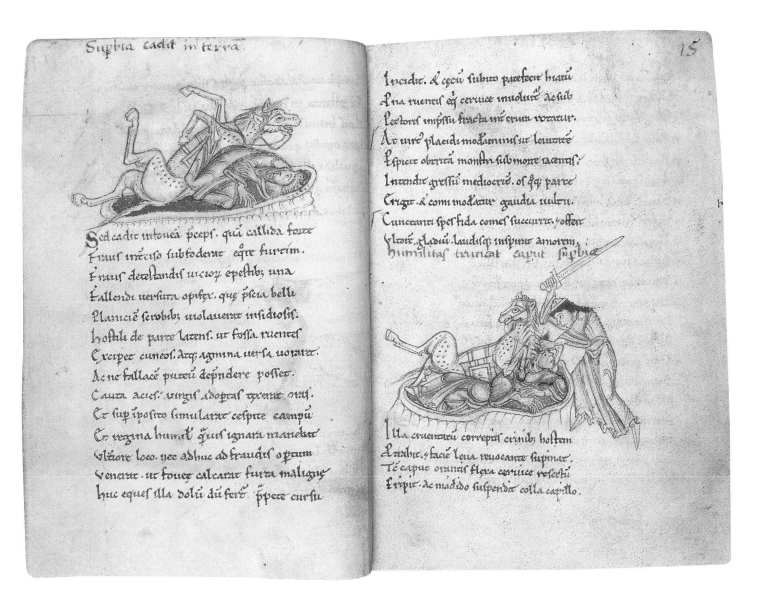

28

Prudentius: 'Psychomachia'

Superbia (Pride) falls into a pit and is then beheaded by Humilitas (Humility)

England, St Albans, *c.*1120.
Latin; 150 x 105 mm, 128 fols.
Cotton MS Titus D. xvi, ff.14b–15

The 'Psychomachia' (or 'Spiritual Combat') is an allegorical poem presenting the struggle between Christianity and paganism as a struggle between the Christian virtues and the pagan vices. Its author was a lawyer and civil servant, born in Spain in 348. The work was extremely popular during the early Middle Ages and this is one of the latest of some 20 surviving illustrated copies. Stylistically its tinted drawings, while looking back to pre-Conquest work, are closely related to the miniatures in the great St Albans Psalter, now in Hildesheim.

29

Silos Apocalypse

St Michael and his angels battling with the dragon

Spain, Silos, 1109.
Latin; 380 x 240 mm, 280 fols.
Additional MS 11695, ff.147b–148

Beatus of Liébana composed his Commentary on the Apocalypse about 776. Such was its popularity within Spain that more than 20 elaborately illustrated copies have come down to us. This example was made in the Benedictine monastery of Silos in northern Spain. Its scribes, working in the distinctive Visigothic script, are named as Dominicus and Nunnio. They had finished their work in 1091. A painter called Petrus was responsible for at least part of the decoration. The entire book was completed in the summer of 1109.

30

Queen Melisende's Psalter

The Harrowing of Hell; the Three Maries at the tomb of Christ

Crusader Kingdom of Jerusalem, 1131–43.
Latin; 215 x 140 mm, 218 fols.
Egerton MS 1139, ff.9b–10

Melisende became queen of the Crusader Kingdom of Jerusalem when her father, Baldwin II, died in 1131. This richly decorated psalter, bound in ivory carved with scenes from the life of David, was made for her in the scriptorium of the Holy Sepulchre. It was illuminated by four artists, all probably westerners but strongly influenced by contemporary Byzantine work. The painter responsible for these and other New Testament scenes signs himself 'Basilius'.

31 (above)

Shaftesbury Psalter

The Almighty dispatching the Archangel Gabriel to make the Annunciation; the Three Maries at the tomb of Christ

England, probably West Country, c.1130–40.
Latin; 220 x 130 mm, 179 fols.
Lansdowne MS 383, ff.12b–13

This relatively small-scale manuscript was designed for private devotional use and presumably first belonged to the woman who is seen kneeling in the margins of two of the pages bearing miniatures. Entries in the calendar suggest that she may have been connected with the Benedictine nunnery at Shaftesbury in Dorset. Stylistically the book is closely related to one of the masterpieces of English Romanesque painting, the St Albans Psalter, which was made about ten years earlier for Christina, anchoress of Markyate, at the order of Abbot Geoffrey of St Albans (1119-47). It is now in Hildesheim.

32 (opposite)

Bible Picture Leaf

Twelve scenes from the Christmas story, from the Annunciation to the Shepherds to the Death of Herod

England, Canterbury, c.1140.
No text; 405 x 300 mm, single leaf.
Additional MS 37472 no.1 (recto)

This is the second of four surviving leaves (now divided between three libraries) which were probably once a part of a particularly grand psalter. Their date and their similarity to the late 12th-century picture leaves in the last of the Utrecht Psalter 'copies', now in Paris, suggest that they could have been from the Eadwine Psalter, now in Trinity College, Cambridge. It was originally the property of Christ Church Cathedral Priory in Canterbury. Carrying scenes from both the Old and the New Testaments, they echo the pages of biblical subjects in the Gospels of St Augustine, traditionally brought to Canterbury by the apostle of England in 597.

33 (above)

Siegburg Epistle Lectionary

The Prophet Isaiah; the Tree of Jesse

Rhineland, Siegburg, *c*.1140–50.
Latin; 270 x 160 mm, 106 fols.
Harley MS 2889, ff. 3b–4

Elaborate gospel lectionaries are comparatively common,
but an illustrated epistle lectionary of this date is a great
rarity. The manuscript contains biblical extracts to be read
at the appropriate point during the celebration of Mass.
These two miniatures introduce the season of Christmas.
The Benedictine abbey of St Michael at Siegburg is about
15 miles south-east of Cologne. This is one of an interesting
group of contemporary books connected with the monastery.

34 (opposite)

Ottobeuren Collectar

The Adoration of the Magi

Swabia, Ottobeuren, second half of the 12th century.
Latin; 290 x 205 mm, 153 fols.
Yates Thompson MS 2, f.62b

Stylistically conservative when compared with other south
German manuscripts of the period, this volume of texts for
the recitation of the divine office was made for the abbey of
Ottobeuren in Swabia in the time of Prior Reinfrid, who died
in or after 1180. It is possible that he was himself the scribe.
It is decorated with 27 miniatures of scenes from the life of
Christ and punctuated with elaborate gold and silver initials
which look back to work of the Ottonian period.

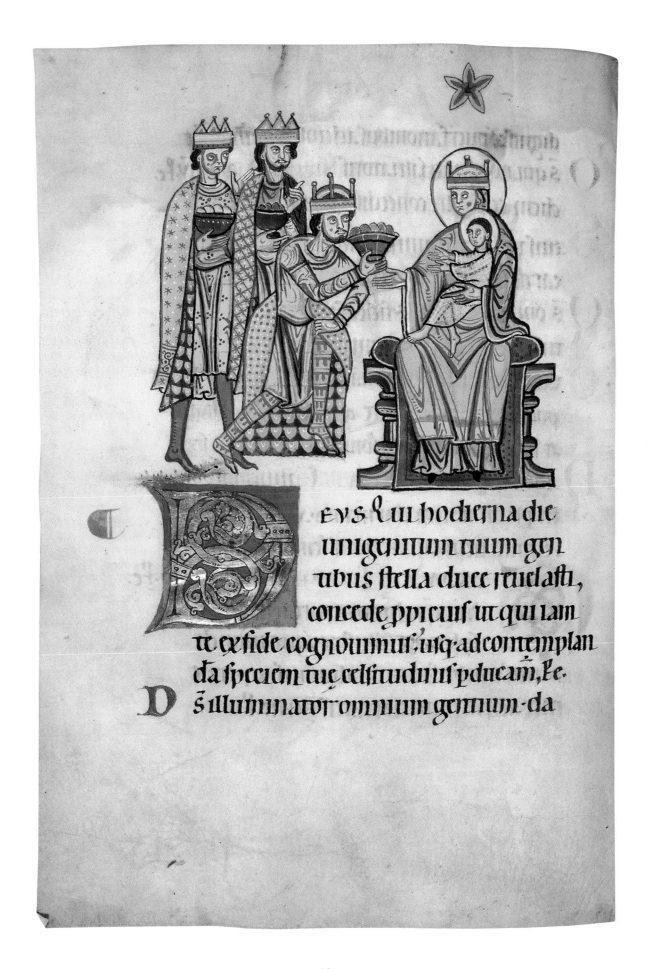

EVS qui hodierna die
unigenitum tuum gen
tibus stella duce reuelasti,
concede ppiciuf ut qui iam
te ex fide cognouimuf, usq; ad contemplan
da specient tue celsitudinis pducam̄, ke.
ſ illuminator omnium gentium · da

35 (above)

Parc Bible

The Virgin and Child

Mosan region, Parc, 1148.
Latin; 430 x 305 mm, 207 fols.
Additional MS 14788, f.207 (detail)

The Premonstratensian abbey of St Mary of Parc, near
Louvain in modern Belgium, owned this bible in three
volumes, the first two of which are dated 1148. This lovely
group of the Virgin and Child appears as an illustration to
the genealogy of Christ which is placed at the end of the
first volume. Physically rather smaller than some of the other
multi-volume bibles of the period, the Parc Bible reflects
influence from both northern France and the Rhineland.

36 (opposite)

Worms Bible I

St Jerome, with the decorated initial to his prologue

Rhineland, Frankenthal, 1148.
Latin; 535 x 353 mm, 301 fols.
Harley MS 2803, f.1b

Traditionally known as the Worms Bible because it
belonged in the 17th century to the church of St Mary
there, this two-volume bible has recently been identified
as a product of the Augustinian monastery of St Mary
Magdalene at Frankenthal, a few miles south of the city.
The hands responsible for its majestic script and exuberant
decoration appear in a number of other manuscripts from the
same source.

INCIPIT·EPLA·SCI·
HIERONIMI·PBRI·
AD·PAVLINV·Q·
PBRM·DE·OMNI
BVS·DIVINE·HIST
ORIE·LIBRIS:

RATER
AMBROSIVS.
tua mihi mu
nuscula pferenſ
detulit. et ſuauiſ
ſimaſ litteraſ que á
principio amicicia
rü fidem pbateiam
fidem et ueteriſ amici
cie pferebant. Vera enim
illa neceſſitudo eſt·et xpi
glutino copulata·quã non
utilitaſ rei familiariſ·ñ pſentia tantũ
corporũ·non ſubdola·et palpanſ adu
latio·ſed dei timor et diuinarũ ſcrip
turarũ ſtudia conciliant·Legimuſ
inueteribuſ hyſtoriiſ quoſdã luſtraſſe

Incipit epła ſ.hieronimi pbri ad paulinũ pbrm ð oib' diuine hiſtorie
libri

51

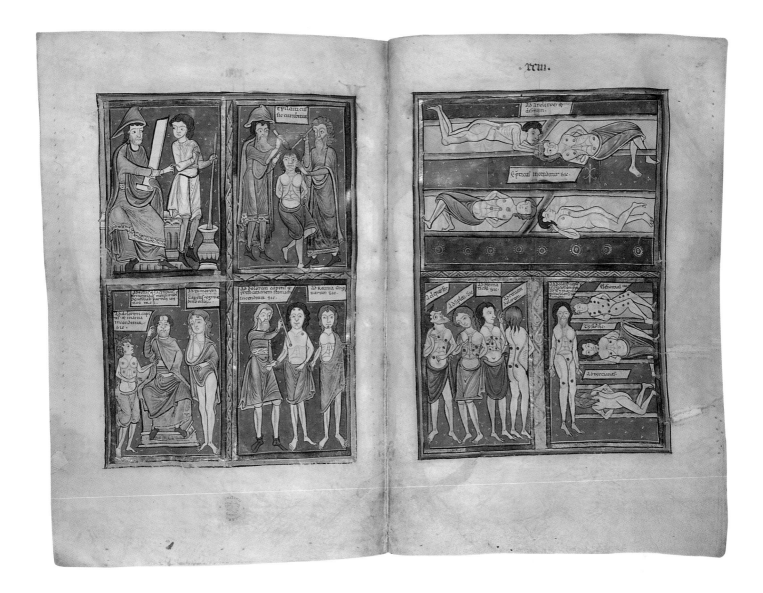

37 (opposite)

Psalter of Henry of Blois

The Annunciation to the Shepherds; the Magi before Herod

England, Winchester, *c*.1150.
Latin and French; 320 x 230 mm, 142 fols.
Cotton MS Nero C. iv, f.11

King Stephen's younger brother, Henry of Blois, Bishop of Winchester 1129–71, is thought to have been the original owner of this grand psalter. It was made in Winchester, perhaps at Hyde Abbey (formerly the New Minster) rather than in the Benedictine cathedral priory itself. It begins with 38 pages of miniatures of subjects from the Old and New Testaments, representing English Romanesque painting at its height, and may be compared with work in wall-painting and enamel as well as with other manuscripts of the period.

38 (above)

Medical and Herbal Collections

Medical miniatures including a guide to cautery points

England, probably the North, last decade of the 12th century.
Latin; 295 x 195 mm, 95 fols.
Sloane MS 1975, ff.91b–92

This is a luxury copy of some of the medical and herbal lore available to the medieval medical practitioner. It probably derives from a 6th-century archetype, perhaps through a copy made before the Norman Conquest. The manuscript includes more than 200 miniatures of plants, together with a number of pictures of animals and birds with medicinal properties. These miniatures, which are stylistically very closely related to northern French work of the period, offer practical information about cauterisation and surgical procedures.

39 (opposite)

Floreffe Bible

Introduction to St John's Gospel; the Ascension

Mosan region, Floreffe, *c*.1156.
Latin; 475 x 330 mm, 256 fols.
Additional MS 17738, f.199

This is the second volume of a great bible made for the Premonstratensian monastery of Floreffe, near Namur in modern Belgium, which was founded in 1121. Each of the four gospels is prefaced by an elaborate typological composition based on an episode from the life of Christ. The manuscript has also been used as a receptacle for a series of historical annals ending in 1156, which provides a probable date for the bible as a whole.

40 (above)

Bestiary

Cat, mouse and weasel

England, *c*.1170.
Latin; 300 x 180 mm, 41 fols.
Additional MS 11283, f.15 (detail)

Bestiaries contain descriptions of birds and beasts, often fabulous but sometimes remarkably accurate, to which Christian moral and allegorical interpretations were applied. They were very popular during the Middle Ages and many beautifully illustrated copies survive, particularly from the 12th and 13th centuries. This is the earliest known example of an expanded version in which the creatures are classified as beasts, birds, reptiles and fish. It is illustrated with lively naturalistic drawings of individual subjects.

41 (overleaf, left)

Arnstein Bible

Opening of St Matthew's Gospel

Rhineland, Arnstein, *c*.1172.
Latin; 540 x 355 mm, 243 fols.
Harley MS 2799, f.155

In January 1721 the Harley library was enriched by the purchase of a substantial group of manuscripts from the Premonstratensian monastery of St Mary and St Nicolas at Arnstein on the river Lahn, not far from its junction with the Rhine at Koblenz. These included the abbey's splendid two-volume bible which, like its sister manuscript from Floreffe, contained a sequence of historical annals (now preserved separately in Darmstadt) ending in 1172 and suggesting a date for the manuscript as a whole. The annals also name the scribe as a monk called Lunandus.

42 (overleaf, right)

Arnstein Passional

The martyrdoms of Saints Peter and Paul

Rhineland, Arnstein, 1170s.
Latin; 550 x 365 mm, 198 fols.
Harley MS 2801, f.21

Also from Arnstein comes a massive three-volume collection of the lives of the saints, decorated in the same style as the bible, with enormous penwork initials composed of exuberant foliage. It contains this single full-page coloured drawing of the deaths of the two principal apostles. The heads of the executioners nailing St Peter to his cross have been obliterated, probably by an indignant devotee.

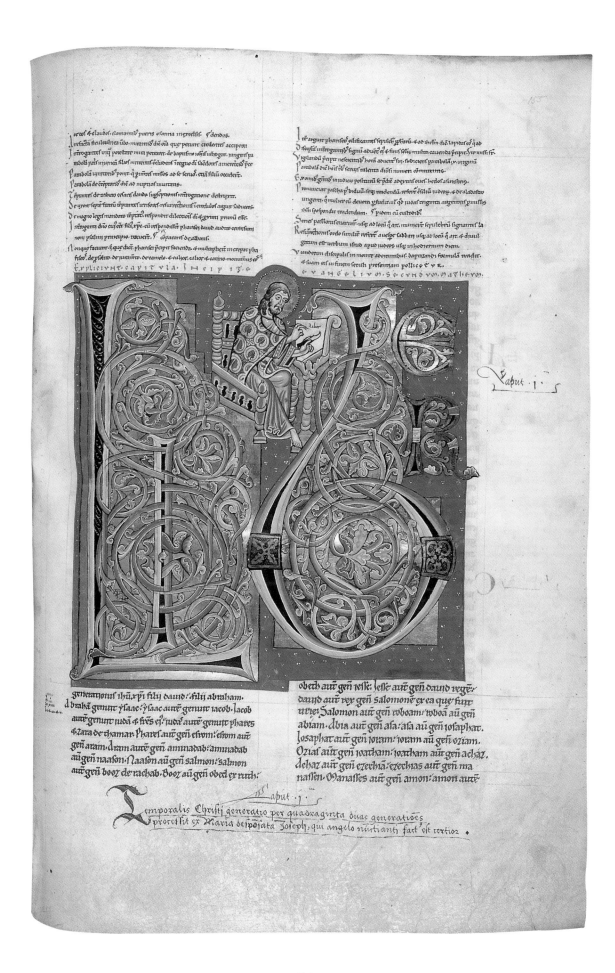

43 (opposite)

Hrabanus Maurus: 'De Laudibus Sancte Crucis'

The Emperor Louis the Pious

Rhineland, Arnstein, 1170s.
Latin; 425 x 330 mm, 52 fols.
Harley MS 3045, f.2

Born about 776 in Mainz, where he eventually became archbishop in 847 after spending the greater part of his life in the monastery of Fulda, Hrabanus Maurus was one of the most prominent teachers and writers of the Carolingian age. This, though not the most profound of his works, was apparently the most popular. It survives in a number of copies, all derived from the 9th-century original which was addressed to Charlemagne's son and heir, Louis the Pious. His name, 'Hludovvicum', may be read on the left-hand side of the halo in this late 12th-century copy.

44 (above)

Scenes from the Life of Christ

The Annunciation

Flanders or north-western France, end of the 12th century.
Latin inscriptions; 230 x 145 mm, 8 detached leaves.
Cotton MS Caligula A. vii, f.3

Painted with great elegance and notable for the exceptional quality and delicacy of their patterned gold backgrounds, these miniatures were probably once part of a richly illuminated psalter. Their place of origin is not apparent but their style is strongly coloured by a knowledge of Byzantine painting and there are also recognisable traces of English influence.

45 (above)

Medical and Herbal Collections

Figures of physicians

Mosan region, *c*.1175.
Latin; 215 x 155 mm, 92 fols.
Harley MS 1585, ff.12b–13

These two fine drawings of physicians appear in a volume
of collected medical and herbal material written in the valley
of the river Meuse, in the general neighbourhood of Liège
in modern Belgium, late in the 12th century. The region was
famed for the quality and range of its goldsmiths' work, to
which these figures are closely related. The man on the
left-hand page is apparently conjuring the earth, giver of
healing plants.

46 (opposite)

Gospels of St Luke and St John

St John writing his Gospel

Germany, possibly Hildesheim, end of the 12th century.
Latin; 325 x 195 mm, 53 fols.
Additional MS 27926, f.28

The evangelist St John is shown both as the author of the
fourth gospel, the opening words of which he is writing, and
as the visionary responsible for the Apocalypse, represented by
figures of the Seven Churches of Asia and by seven candle-
sticks. His traditional eagle symbol occupies the initial I,
between figures of Christ and of the Virgin and Child.
The manuscript, which was intended to be used for gospel
readings at Mass and which still has a medieval binding, once
belonged to the nunnery of Heiningen in the diocese of
Hildesheim.

verbū. Et uerbū erat apud dm̄. Et ds̄ erat
uerbū. Hoc erat inprincipio apud dm̄.
Omia p̄ipsū facta sū. & sine ipso factū est
nichil. Quod factū est. inipso uita erat.
Et uita erat lux hominū. & lux intenebs̄
lucet. et tenebre eam non cōprehendert.
Fuit homo missus a dō. cui nomen erat io
hannes. Hic uenit intestimoniū ut testi
moniū p̄hiberet de lumine: ut om̄s cre
derent p̄illū. Non erat ille lux. sed ut tes
timoniū p̄hiberet de lumine: Erat lux
uera. que̅ illuminat omne̅ homine̅ ue
niente̅ in hunc mundū. In mundo erat
& mundus p̄ipsū factus est. & mundus
eū non cognouit. In ppria uenit. & sui
eū non recepunt. Quotqt au̅ recepunt eū

47

La Charité Psalter

King David pursued by his sons

France, La Charité-sur-Loire, end of the 12th century.
Latin; 255 x 160 mm, 93 fols.
Harley MS 2895, f.81b (detail)

The scriptorium of the Cluniac priory of La Charité-sur-Loire in western France produced this exceptionally elegant psalter, which later belonged to the Benedictine nunnery of the Holy Cross in Poitiers. The book's historiated initials look forward to the softer style of the 13th century. Each psalm originally began with a large decorated letter, often enclosing a biblical scene, but many of these have been cut out, probably during the 17th century.

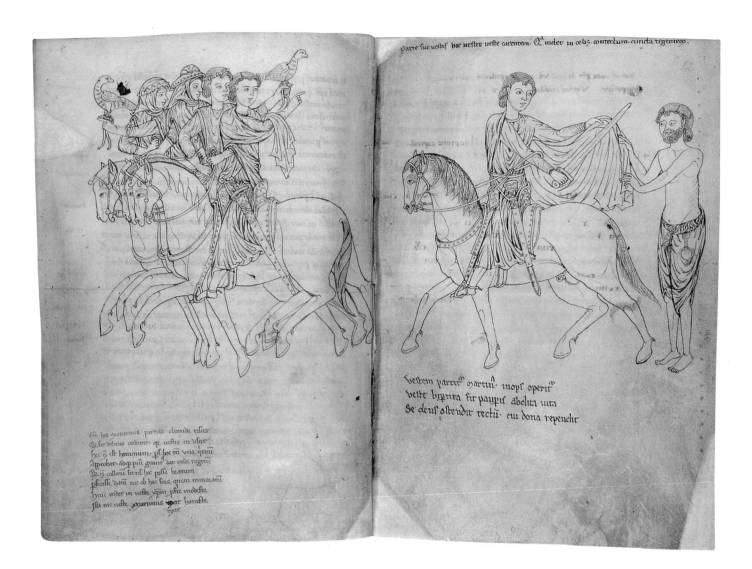

48

Theological Tracts

St Martin and the beggar

Southern Netherlands, Tournai, *c.*1200.
Latin; 230 x 155 mm, 93 fols.
Additional MS 15219, ff.11b–12

This drawing of St Martin leaving his hunting companions in order to divide his cloak with a beggar bears no relationship to the textual content of the manuscript in which it appears. It was inserted to honour the patron saint of the monastery to which the book belonged. The artist is particularly notable for the loving care with which he has depicted the costumes and accessories of the figures. His style is closely related to that of the goldsmiths' work of the time, personified by the great Nicolas of Verdun.

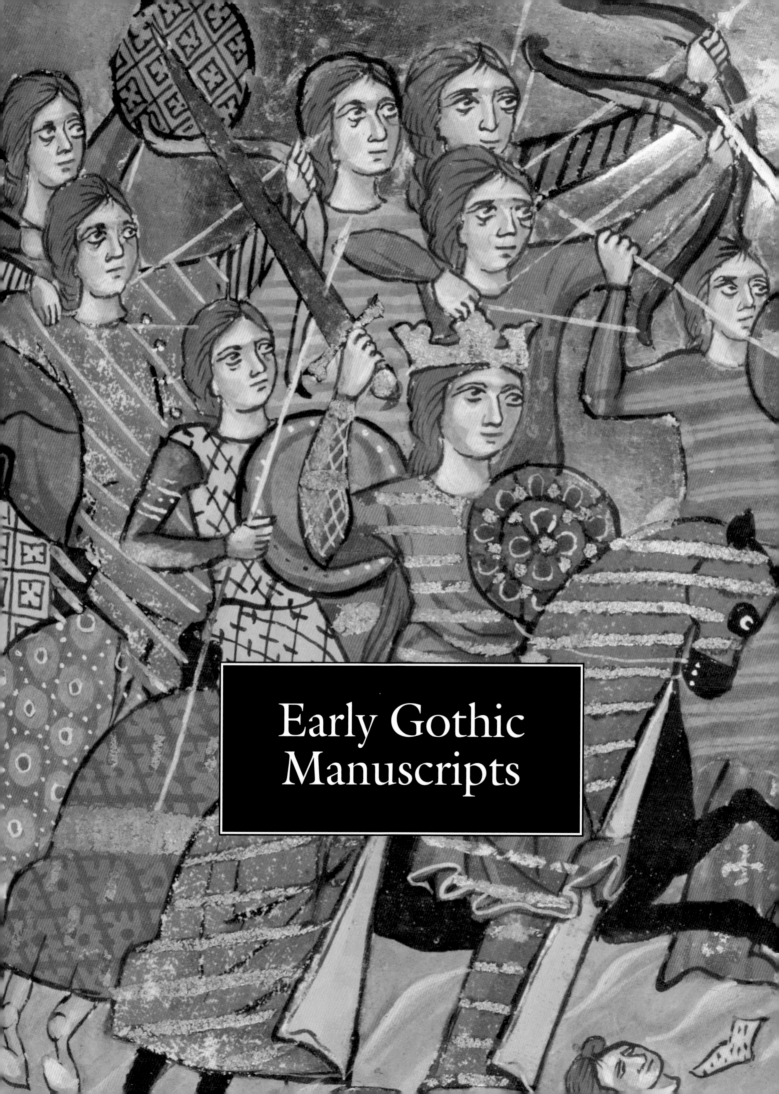

Early Gothic
Manuscripts

Astylistic transition from Romanesque to Gothic took place gradually during the latter part of the 12th century. The building of the cathedral of Chartres, its west front erected during the third quarter of the century, was a major landmark in the process. Many further wonderful churches, including the French cathedrals of Reims and Amiens and the English cathedral of Salisbury, were to be built during the ensuing hundred years. Contemporary masterpieces of illumination were mainly devotional and include a large number of lavishly decorated psalters from workshops all over Europe. Although the personal names of their original owners are in most cases unknown, it is frequently possible to identify with some precision the place in which a book was designed to be used (50, 67) or the status of the person who used it. Such owners included an abbot of the Benedictine abbey of Evesham (63), a nun in a community in Nantes (57) and, possibly, the papal representative in England during the 1260s (69).

The psalter was the basis of all regular devotion, both communal and personal. The Rule of St Benedict, drawn up in Italy in the early 6th century and thereafter the foundational text of western monasticism, lays down very precise directions for the use of the psalms in daily worship, dividing them between the eight services of the office in such a way as to ensure the recitation of the complete psalter during the course of each week. It is not uncommon for manuscripts to include in their decoration a sequence of elaborate initials marking these divisions. Many of them also include series of miniatures of episodes from the Bible, after the fashion of the Tiberius Psalter (16) and the Psalter of Henry of Blois (37) in earlier periods, together with decorated calendars which commonly include small scenes of the occupations of the months, offering graphic evidence for the study of contemporary everyday life. The feast days of local saints appear in calendars and litanies, providing clues not only to the destinations of individual books but also sometimes to their places of manufacture.

A commercial book trade was well established by the middle of the 13th century in such centres as Paris and Oxford, where its development had been encouraged not merely by the presence of suitable patrons but also by the growth of the universities, the earliest of which came into being during the late 12th century. Surviving local records have revealed the existence of streets or clusters of houses apparently given over almost completely to the production of manuscripts and documents, with scribes, illuminators, parchment makers and bookbinders living alongside each other in the pursuit of their communal craft. In Oxford they carried on their trade in Catte Street and one of the householders, W. de Brailes, can be identified with several existing illuminated manuscripts because he was sufficiently proud of his work to have taken the unusual step of putting his name to some of his

Detail from figure 72

miniatures. Although by comparison with the work of some of his most sophisticated contemporaries, such as the genius who produced the Evesham crucifixion miniature (63), his paintings appear somewhat naive, he has a two-fold significance. Precisely identified and localised, he was also responsible for the earliest surviving example of an individual book of hours (55), a type of devotional book that was to grow in popularity over the next two or three hundred years until it merited description as the biggest bestseller of the Middle Ages.

Alongside commercial book production, which was largely a secular activity, books continued to be produced within religious communities. It is not unlikely that the wonderfully eccentric psalter from the diocese of Bamberg (74) was made within the nunnery for which it was intended. In England the Benedictine abbey of St Albans housed one of the major monastic figures of the 13th century, the chronicler, author, cartographer, scribe and artist Matthew Paris. Probably born about the beginning of the century, Matthew Paris entered the religious life on 21 January 1217 and thereafter until his death in 1259 only rarely left the shelter of his abbey, though he himself tells us that he was present at one or two notable events, such as the translation of the relics of St Thomas Becket at Canterbury in July 1220 and the marriage of Henry III and Eleanor of Provence at Westminster in 1236. He also paid a brief visit to Norway in 1248 to settle an ecclesiastical dispute on behalf of the pope. His very wide circle of acquaintance, which included not only members of the royal family but also representatives of the royal council and many of the leading churchmen of the day, assured him of the very best and most immediate sources of information for his historical writings, the most important of which is the 'Chronica Maiora' (59).

The events which he was able to describe from the first-hand evidence of his friends represented a stirring period of European history. In England at the beginning of the century King John lost his continental lands in Normandy and Poitou to King Philip Augustus of France and found himself obliged to accept the demands of his barons and affix his seal of assent to Magna Carta at Runnymede in June 1215. Two major saints whose names remain familiar to this day, the Italian St Francis (died 1226) and the Spanish St Dominic (died 1221), laid the foundations of their respective orders which, encouraged by the patronage of the royalty and nobility of Europe, were quickly to move into an extremely influential position within the church. Farther afield the Fourth Crusade (1202–1204), deflected from its true objectives by the ambitions of the Venetians, had resulted in the sack of Constantinople by the western allies and the establishment of a short-lived Latin Empire of the east, which did more than all the onslaughts of Islam to weaken the old Byzantine Empire. In 1240 the Latin Emperor Baldwin sold to the French King Louis IX one of the major relics of the Christian faith, the True Crown of Thorns. It was to contain this treasure that the Sainte Chapelle in Paris, one of the supreme jewels of Gothic architecture, was constructed during the 1240s. Matthew Paris's chronicle records, with appropriate marginal illustrations, much of the subsequent history of the Holy Land within his own lifetime, placing particular emphasis upon the expedition led in 1240 by Henry III's young brother, Richard of Cornwall, who probably provided the information personally.

Louis IX of France, raised to the altar as a saint in 1297, led the last two crusades. He died in Tunis during his second campaign, diverted into Africa to further the ambitions of his brother, Charles of Anjou, to found a Mediterranean Empire centred on Sicily, which Charles had taken in 1266. Prince Edward of England was to have joined him in this crusade. Before his accession to the English throne in 1272, he did spend almost two years in the Holy Land, where his experiences of crusader military architecture probably influenced his own subsequent castle building in Wales. In 1291 the city of Acre finally fell to the forces of Islam amid scenes of horrendous carnage in which the great majority of the Latin population perished, marking the end of the crusader kingdoms of the east.

The career of the versatile Matthew Paris also reflects another aspect of the literary activities of the 13th century. Alongside his lively and valuable Latin historical writings, he produced several shorter works in French verse, narrating the lives of saints such as Alban and Thomas Becket for the personal use of members of his circle, which included several high-born and clearly literate ladies. An increasing and widespread use of the vernacular as a vehicle for literary work is a significant development of the period throughout Europe. The 'Roman de la Rose' (190), most celebrated of all works in medieval French, was composed at this time. Left unfinished by Guillaume de Lorris about 1237, it was completed some 40 years later by Jean de Meun. French was also used in historical narratives such as the 'Histoire Universelle' (72) or for notes accompanying illustrations of the kings of England (75). In Spain, where Castile and Leon had been united under one rule in 1230, both literary and legal materials (73) were written in the vernacular at the court of Alfonso X, who was the half-brother of Edward I's queen, Eleanor of Castile.

In England, where French remained the standard language of the cultured classes, a vernacular literature was slower to blossom. Most people are however probably familiar with the famous medieval English song, 'Sumer is icumen in', which survives in a single copy apparently written at the abbey of Reading about the middle of the 13th century. The period also produced Layamon's 'Brut' – the earliest lengthy poem in Middle English. It recounts legendary British history from the time of the Trojans, supposed ancestors of the race to the defeat of the Britons by the Saxons after the death of King Arthur, in some 16,000 lines. The Arthurian legend was to become an enduring feature of the literature of the later Middle Ages and found concrete expression in the spring of 1278, when the supposed tomb of Arthur and Guinevere at Glastonbury Abbey was opened in the presence of Edward and his queen, who personally carried the relics to their new resting place.

49 (opposite)

Psalter

The Last Supper

Germany, Thuringia or Saxony, beginning of the
13th century.
Latin; 250 x 180 mm, 168 fols.
Additional MS 18144, f.13

Because the text of the psalms provided the foundation of
daily worship, both public and private, richly illuminated
psalters were frequently made for the use of individual
patrons. The principal divisions of their text are commonly
marked by decorated initials and many of the manuscripts
begin with sequences of scenes from the life of Christ. This
fine example from Germany is closely related to a psalter, now
preserved at Cividale in northern Italy, which traditionally
belonged to St Elizabeth of Hungary, wife of the Landgrave
of Thuringia, who died in 1331.

50 (above)

Westminster Psalter

David as a musician; Beatus initial

England, possibly St Albans or Winchester, *c*.1200.
Latin; 230 x 160 mm, 224 fols.
Royal MS 2 A. xxii, ff.14b–15

Written to accord with the liturgical requirements of
Westminster Abbey, this very accomplished psalter contains
five full-page miniatures, the last of which portrays David
crowned and enthroned in the guise of a medieval king. On
the opposite page the psalter text opens with a magnificent
initial B, filled with animal and plant life and edged with
further scenes from David's story, including the slaying of
Goliath. The royal abbey of Westminster, closely associated
with the court, has been the traditional place of coronation of
England's kings since the time of William the Conqueror.

51 (right)

Bede's Prose Life of St Cuthbert

News of the saint's death is signalled to his brethren

England, Durham, *c.*1200.
Latin; 135 x 100 mm, 150 fols.
Yates Thompson MS 26, f.74b

St Cuthbert, whose relics are enshrined in Durham cathedral, is the most important saint of the north of England. A member of the monastic community of Lindisfarne, of which he was bishop during the last few years of his life, he chose to spend his final weeks in his hermitage on the North Sea island of Inner Farne. He died on the night of 20 March 687 and news of his passing was signalled by torches to the waiting monks on the Holy Island of Lindisfarne, some six miles away. In this unusual scene the relative positions of the two islands are correctly shown, making it one of the earliest known topographical drawings.

52 (opposite, below)

Giraldus Cambrensis: 'Topographica Hibernia'

The legend of the wolf that talked with the priest of Ulster

Southern England, *c*.1220.
Latin; 275 x 195 mm, 147 fols.
Royal MS 13 B. viii, ff.17b–18 (detail)

In 1185 Giraldus Cambrensis (Gerald of Wales), chaplain to King Henry II, accompanied Prince John on a visit to Ireland. On his return he dedicated to the king an account of his observations, enlivened by descriptions of animals and birds and by the inclusion of stories which he had heard. This copy of his work, which dates from the early years of the 13th century, was probably made before his death in 1220. It also contains an account of his journey through Wales in 1188, in the company of Baldwin, Archbishop of Canterbury.

53 (above)

Bestiary

The goat and the bull

Northern England, probably Durham, *c*.1200–10.
Latin; 225 x 160 mm, 112 fols.
Royal MS 12 C. xix, ff.31b–32

Stylistically very close to the richly illustrated Life of St Cuthbert (51), this manuscript was probably also produced at Durham. It contains 80 miniatures of beasts, birds and reptiles, most of which are set off by gold grounds within coloured frames. The animals themselves are more realistically portrayed than those in some earlier bestiaries. Although this remains a work of reference and instruction, it is also quite clearly an expensive and luxurious product in which its owner could take great pride.

54

Psalter and Hours

The Entry into Jerusalem; the Last Supper; Christ washing the feet of the Disciples; Christ awakening Peter, James and John in the Garden of Gethsemane

England, probably Oxford, *c.*1200–10.
Latin; 295 x 195 mm, 185 fols.
Arundel MS 157, ff.8b–9

This richly decorated book is one of a number of closely related psalters which probably represent the output of a group of professional scribes and illuminators working to order for individual patrons. The saints' days included in their calendars suggest that the group may have been located in Oxford, already by this time a celebrated centre of learning. The manuscript has 20 pages of scenes from the life of Christ, painted in a very lively and dramatic narrative style.

55

De Brailes Hours

David penitent, being birched by a priest

England, Oxford, *c*.1240.
Latin; 150 x 125 mm, 105 fols.
Additional MS 49999, f.72 (detail)

A number of English 13th-century psalters include the Hours
of the Virgin among their supplementary devotions but this
small book is the earliest known English example of a book of
hours produced as a separate entity in its own right. It was
illuminated by an artist who signs himself 'W. de Brailes' and
who is thought to have been the William de Brailes who lived
in Catte Street in Oxford about 1230–60. His idiosyncratic
style has been recognised in a number of other manuscripts.

56

Detached Leaf from a Psalter

Joseph warned by an angel to flee into Egypt

Germany, probably Würzburg, *c*.1240.
Latin; 175 x 135 mm, one of a series of 20 detached leaves.
Additional MS 17687 C

This unusual subject forms part of a sequence of scenes from
the life of Christ which must once have been part of a psalter.
So far 20 leaves from the series have been identified, 16 of
them in the British Library. Originally their versos were blank
but portions of a breviary were added to them early in the
15th century. The heavily modelled draperies, edged with
jagged folds, are very characteristic of South German
illumination of the period.

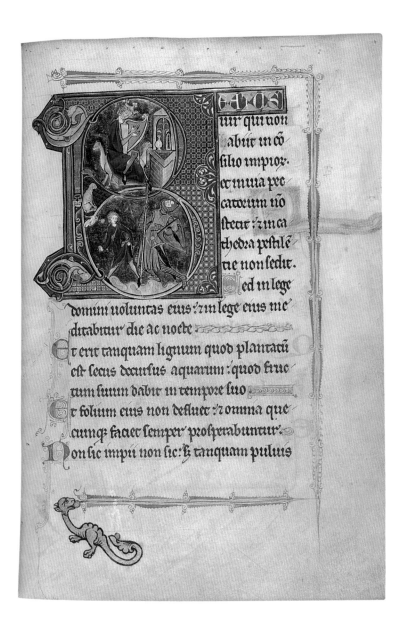

57 (above)

Psalter

David as a musician; David and Goliath

France, Paris, mid 13th century.
Latin; 255 x 175 mm, 182 fols.
Royal MS 2 B. ii, f.7

Two standard scenes from the life of King David are enclosed within the Beatus initial of this psalter which was made in one of the many workshops of mid-13th-century Paris, apparently for the use of a nun in Nantes. At this time, during the reign of Louis IX, Paris was widely famed for the excellence of its illuminators, who attracted customers from far outside the city. Like Oxford, its university supported an extensive book trade which was by no means confined to liturgical materials.

58 (opposite)

Missal

Christ in Majesty

Germany, probably Würzburg, second quarter of the 13th century.
Latin; 210 x 140 mm, 223 fols.
Arundel MS 156, f.99b

The missal contains in a single volume all the various liturgical texts required for the celebration of Mass. This manuscript seems to have been intended for use at the Benedictine abbey church of Komburg in the diocese of Würzburg. The priest who would have used it is shown in his Mass vestments, kneeling at the feet of Christ, who is enthroned within a rainbow and flanked by the traditional symbols of the four evangelists, Matthew's man, Mark's lion, Luke's bullock and John's eagle.

59

Matthew Paris: 'Historia Anglorum' and 'Chronica Maiora III'

The Virgin and Child with the artist

England, St Albans, 1250–9.
Latin; 360 x 250 mm, 232 fols.
Royal MS 14 C. vii, f.6

Matthew Paris, monk of the Benedictine house of St Albans, where he lived from 1217 until his death in 1259, was the most celebrated chronicler of the age. He was also an accomplished craftsman, working in precious metals as well as in paint. This magnificent tinted drawing of the Virgin and Child is placed before a series of drawings of the kings of England in the 'Historia Anglorum'. The artist himself is depicted kneeling in the lower margin, fully identified by name.

60

Matthew Paris: 'Historia Anglorum'

King Henry III sailing to Brittany

England, St Albans, 1250–9.
Latin; 360 x 250 mm, 232 fols.
Royal MS 14 C. vii, f.116b (detail)

The historical writings of Matthew Paris are enlivened by
marginal pictures of the people and events described. This
page is written out in his own very recognisable hand and the
tiny drawing is equally characteristic. Although he seldom left
his abbey, he had a wide circle of acquaintance in the very
highest levels of society, many of whom were frequent visitors
to St Albans, a convenient staging post on the road from
London to the north. From them he obtained first-hand
information about events of the day, all duly incorporated in
his work.

61

Detached Leaf from a Psalter

Scenes from the story of Samson

Germany, upper Rhineland, mid 13th century.
No text; 170 x 120 mm, single leaf.
Additional MS 17864 A

In these two somewhat bloodthirsty scenes, Samson is seen
overcoming the lion and laying about the Philistines with the
jawbone of an ass. His long hair, subsequently cut off by
Delilah, is prominently featured. Three further leaves from
this manuscript are known. One, with scenes from the story
of David, is in the British Library. The book was probably
produced on the borders of what is now Switzerland.

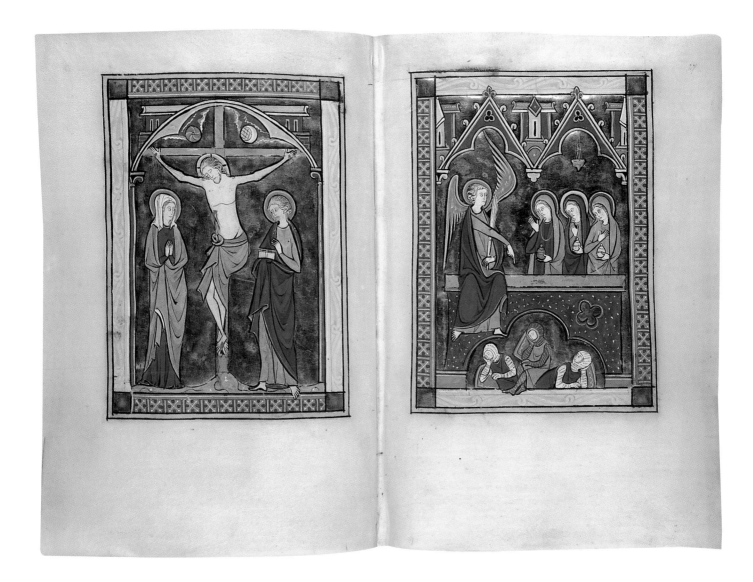

62 (above)

Psalter

The Crucifixion; the Three Maries at the tomb

France, Paris, 1250s.
Latin; 215 x 145 mm, 197 fols.
Additional MS 17868, ff.26b–27

Designed for private use, this luxuriously decorated psalter was made in one of the leading Parisian workshops of the day. Saints named in the calendar suggest that the original owner was connected with north-eastern France. The three soldiers, who have been guarding Christ's sepulchre, are wearing contemporary mail of a type that might have been seen on members of the crusading armies that accompanied St Louis IX on his expeditions to the Holy Land.

63 (opposite)

Evesham Psalter

The Crucifixion

England, Worcester region, c.1250–60.
Latin; 315 x 210 mm, 284 fols.
Additional MS 44874, f.6

The original owner of the manuscript is shown kneeling in the border at the foot of the cross. He was an abbot of the Benedictine monastery of Evesham but the uncertain date of the book does not allow him to be fully identified. An added coat of arms on another page does however suggest that the psalter later passed into the hands of Richard of Cornwall, King of the Romans (died 1272), the younger brother of King Henry III. This miniature is one of the major master-pieces of English Gothic painting. Comparison with work produced earlier in the century suggests that the artist was aware of recent continental developments. The treatment of the draperies is distinctly reminiscent of German work.

64

Rutland Psalter

David and his musicians

England, possibly London, *c.*1260.
Latin; 285 x 200 mm, 193 fols.
Additional MS 62925, ff.97b–98

Six large miniatures and nine historiated initials mark the
liturgical divisions of the text in this outstanding book. Its
marginal decoration, which often appears to be frivolous and
is generally unconnected with the psalms, includes scenes of
everyday life, animals, monsters, grotesques and subjects from
mythology. This type of ornament became increasingly
fashionable on both sides of the Channel during the late 13th
and early 14th centuries and this is apparently the first major
example of it in English illumination. In the miniature on the
left-hand page, King David is shown playing a contemporary
organ. It is pumped by a young man treading bellows, while a
second figure plays a hurdy-gurdy.

65

Apocalypse

The destruction of the Great Whore of Babylon; the marriage feast of the Lamb

England, possibly London, *c.*1260.
Latin; 290 x 220 mm, 38 fols.
Additional MS 35166, ff.22b–23

This is a fine example of the illustrated apocalypse manuscripts that enjoyed a sudden popularity in the mid 13th century, particularly in England. Typically they contain sequences of miniatures showing episodes from the Book of Revelation, sometimes accompanied by scenes from the life of its author, St John the Evangelist, together with the biblical text and a commentary. They were aimed not only at clerics but also at educated lay folk. The earliest examples have been associated with St Albans, but this copy may come from a workshop in London or Westminster and its style suggests the influence of contemporary French work.

Qui retribuunt mala pro bonis detrahebant mi:
qm sequebar bonitatem.
Ne dereliquas me domine deus meus: ne discesseris
a me. Ctis mee.
Intende in adiutorium meum: domine deus salu

meas: ut non delinquam in lingua mea.
Posui ori meo custodiam: cum consisteret pecror
aduersum me.
Obmutui et humiliatus sum et silui a bonis: et
dolor meus renouatus est.

Don auertaf faciem tuam a me:in qua
cumq; die tribulor inclina ad me
aurem tuam.
Inquacumq; die inuocauero te uelo

66 (opposite)

Lyre Psalter

David killing the bear and the lion that
threatened his flocks

Normandy, Lyre, second half of the 13th century.
Latin; 300 x 210 mm, 263 fols.
Additional MS 16975, f.52b (detail)

All the decoration in this manuscript, comprising calendar
miniatures, full-page scenes from the Old and New
Testaments, and historiated initials at the main divisions of
the psalter text, is carried out in tinted outline, in predomi-
nant shades of green and mauve. The book was made for use
at the Benedictine abbey of Lyre in Normandy and its calendar includes commemorations of many of the abbots and
benefactors of the community. Among the latter are the
names of early earls and countesses of Leicester, whose family
came originally to England from Normandy.

67 (above)

York Psalter

Judith beheading Holofernes

England, *c.*1260.
Latin; 345 x 240 mm, 193 fols.
Additional MS 54179, f.95 (detail)

It is clear from the inclusion in its calendar of a number of
feasts characteristic of the diocese of York that this manuscript
was made for a patron connected with the north of England.
There is, however, no evidence to suggest that it was actually
made in the York area and it is more likely that it was ordered
from a workshop in the south of England. Main divisions in
the text are marked by large initials enclosing a mixture of
Old and New Testament subjects. The calendar is ornamented with a series of illustrations of the signs of the zodiac and
the labours of the months.

68

Bible of William of Devon

Opening pages of Genesis

England, perhaps Oxford, *c*.1260–70.
Latin; 315 x 200 mm, 582 fols.
Royal MS 1 D. i, ff.4b–5

The kneeling cleric at the foot of the left-hand page is probably intended to represent the scribe of this book, who signed himself as William of Devon. Unfortunately, he cannot be more exactly identified. In the elaborate frontispiece, figures of Sts Peter, Paul and Martin surround the seated Virgin and Child, above whom is placed the Crucifixion and, in the topmost register, the Coronation of the Virgin. The text of Genesis opens with a large initial enclosing scenes from the story of the Creation.

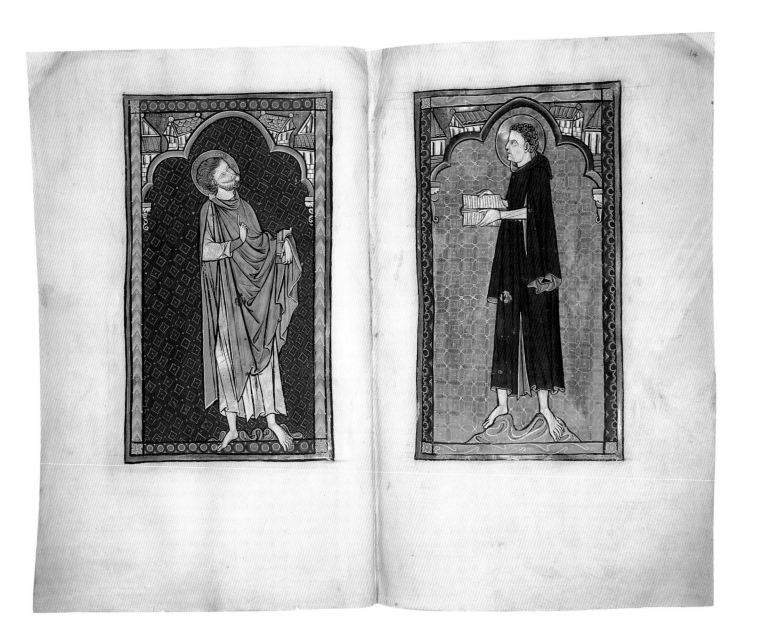

69

Oscott Psalter

Two apostles

England, perhaps Oxford, *c.*1265–70.
Latin and French; 300 x 200 mm, 257 fols.
Additional MS 50000, ff.13b–14

The Oscott Psalter, so named because it belonged during the 19th century to St Mary's College at Oscott, stands equal with the Rutland Psalter (64) as the most elaborate example of English 13th-century illumination. Even its text is written out in red, blue and gold. The book includes 22 full-page miniatures, showing scenes from the life of Christ and standing figures of the apostles, which originally appeared in facing pairs. They have been compared to similar figures on the beautiful but damaged retable in Westminster Abbey. The original owner must have been of very high rank. One candidate is Cardinal Ottobuono Fieschi, afterwards Pope Adrian V, who was papal legate in England between 1265 and 1268.

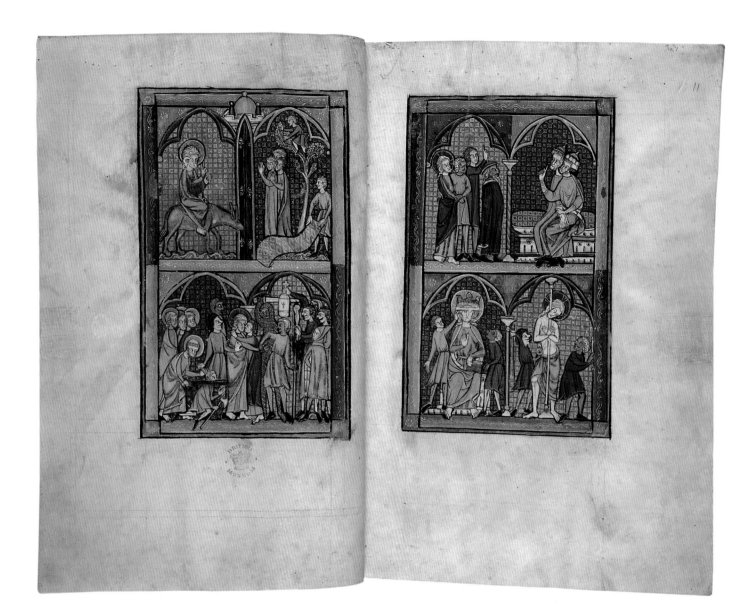

70 (above)

Huth Psalter

Scenes from Christ's Passion: the entry into Jerusalem and the arrest of Christ; Christ before Caiaphas; Christ mocked and scourged

England, Lincoln or York, after 1280.
Latin; 235 x 160 mm, 174 fols.
Additional MS 38116, ff.l0b–11

The inclusion in its calendar of the Translation and Deposition of St Hugh of Lincoln places this manuscript after 1280 and suggests an origin in the neighbourhood of Lincoln itself. A number of Christ's opponents are given dark complexions and exaggeratedly Jewish features, serving to remind the viewer of the very strong anti-Jewish feeling rife in late 13th-century England, culminating in the expulsion of Jews from the kingdom by Edward I in 1290.

71 (opposite)

Salvin Hours

Christ before Pilate

England, diocese of Lincoln, possibly Oxford, *c.*1270.
Latin; 320 x 220 mm, 128 fols.
Additional MS 48985, f.32b

This early book of hours, lavishly produced on the large scale more usually associated with psalters, shares something of the rather flat style seen in the Huth Psalter (70) which goes back ultimately to the work of William de Brailes (55). Here too the figures dragging Christ into the presence of Pilate are given exaggeratedly Jewish features. The original owner of the book is not known but from at least the end of the 17th century it belonged to the Salvin family of County Durham, from which it takes its name.

72

'Histoire Universelle'

Battle between Pyrrhus and Penthesilea, Queen of the Amazons

Crusader Kingdom of Jerusalem, Acre, *c*.1286.
French; 370 x 250 mm, 314 fols.
Additional MS 15268, f.123 (detail)

The 'Histoire Universelle', a popular and widely circulated world chronicle covering the whole of history from the Creation to the rise of Julius Caesar, was compiled in France early in the 13th century. This manuscript is the finest of three comparatively early copies made in the crusader kingdoms of the Holy Land, probably in the scriptorium of St-Jean-d'Acre. It has been suggested that it was a presentation copy designed for Henry II, crowned King of Jerusalem at Tyre in 1286, possibly as a gift on that occasion. The book must date from before the fall of Acre in 1291, when the forces of the west were expelled amid scenes of horrifying carnage.

Sant agostin establecio prime ramiente en la eglesia q̃ nungun clerigo no ouiesse ṗṗrio. E los q̃ lo quisiessen auer q̃ no los teuiessen por seer clerigos. Mas q̃ uiuiessen en cada logar todos en uno ⁊ lo q̃ ouiessen fuesse comunalmientre de to.

73

Law Code of Alfonso X, King of Castile and Leon

The provision of payment for the clergy

Spain, Castile or Leon, last quarter of the 13th century.
Spanish; 360 x 240 mm, 120 fols.
Additional MS 20787, f.112b (detail)

Nicknamed El Sabio ('The Learned'), Alfonso X, who reigned between 1252 and 1284, was renowned for his interest in books and scholarship. This is the earliest known copy of the first part ('Primera Partida') of a comprehensive legal code which he drew up, dealing with ecclesiastical matters and covering all aspects of religious life. Here the clergy are shown receiving payment in money and in kind. A workshop under Alfonso's own patronage produced a succession of illuminated manuscripts, including several copies of the 'Cantigas' in honour of the Virgin Mary which the king collected throughout his life. The script and decoration in this book are closely related to the work of his craftsmen, suggesting that it too was probably made in the royal workshop, perhaps even within his lifetime.

74 (opposite)

Psalter

Jacob's ladder

Germany, diocese of Bamberg, late 13th century.
Latin; 230 x 165 mm, 170 fols.
Additional MS 60629, f.87b

This psalter, richly decorated with eight full-page miniatures and a sequence of historiated text initials, was made for the use of a Benedictine nunnery apparently in the diocese of Bamberg. Its style, though somewhat crude and almost child-ish, is very arresting in its use of brilliant primary colours and large areas of thick burnished gold. Here the figure of Jacob, lying dreaming as angels ascend and descend the ladder, is surrounded by vignettes of men and animals, hunting or playing musical instruments. At the beginning of the 16th century the manuscript belonged to Dorothea, daughter of the Margrave Albert Achilles of Brandenburg and abbess of the Poor Clares at Bamberg.

75 (above)

Miscellaneous Chronicles

William of Normandy killing Harold at the Battle of Hastings

England, *c.*1280–1300.
French; approximately 205 x 155 mm (damaged by the Cotton Library fire of 1731), 101 fols.
Cotton MS Vitellius A. xiii, f.3b

This is one of eight large miniatures of the kings of England from Edward the Confessor to Edward I, in whose reign they were painted. Each king is characterised by a short descriptive text in French, decoratively written in red, blue and gold. In this military scene the opposing forces are arrayed in the arms and armour of the 13th century; heraldic charges more appropriate to the time of Edward I than to that of William I add colour to the design. A pleasing touch is the small group of men in everyday dress clearing up the aftermath of the battle beneath the feet of the mounted knights.

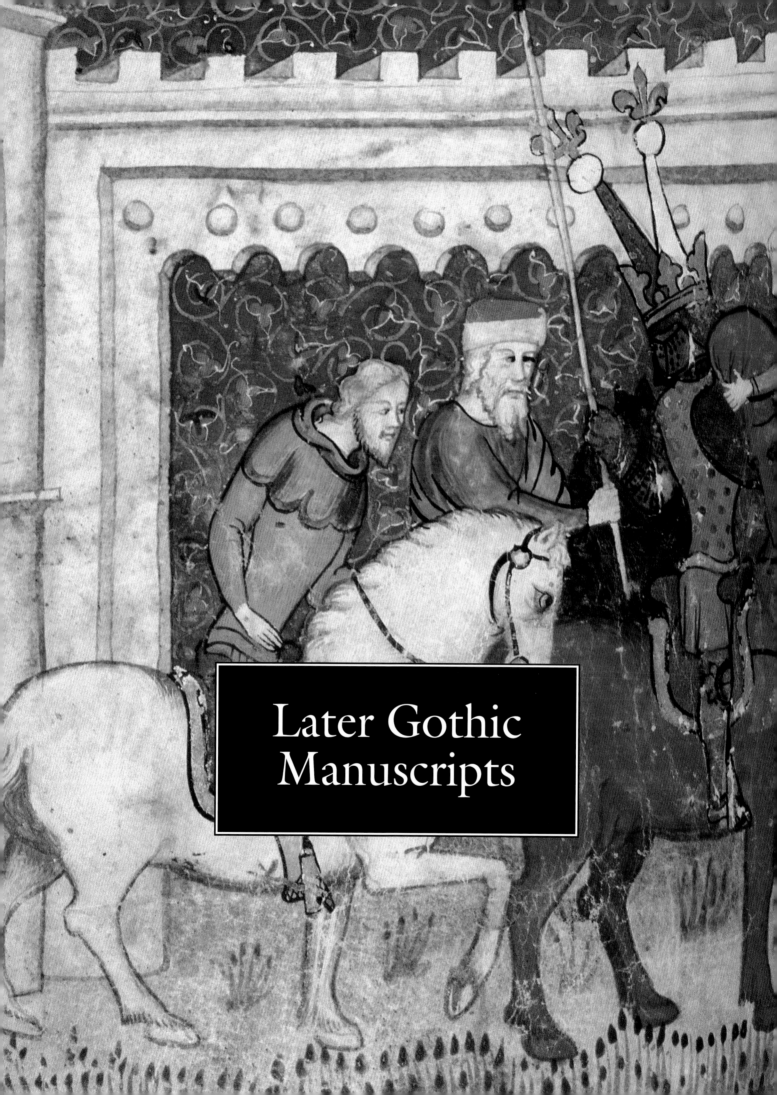

Later Gothic Manuscripts

During the late 13th and early 14th centuries English and French styles of book painting are very visibly interdependent and their joint influence was widely felt in other parts of Europe, including the Low Countries (83), Switzerland (81) and Italy (96). Historians of medieval art have in general been inclined to award pre-eminence to France and to the achievements of Parisian illuminators of the time of St Louis IX, but some of the English manuscripts, notably the Oscott Psalter (69), have a characteristic monumentality that is lacking in French work. The two kingdoms were of course very closely linked in many respects, not least in their geographical proximity, divided only by a narrow stretch of sea which might be regarded more as a potential highway than as a physical barrier, given the general circumstances of medieval travel. For English travellers with destinations in Italy, the Spanish peninsula or any part of the Mediterranean, the bulk of France had to be either traversed or circumvented on the way. However, the massive areas in western France that had been controlled during the 12th century by Henry II of England were quickly dissipated by his 13th-century successors, save for the Duchy of Aquitaine for which Henry III agreed to pay feudal homage to Louis IX, an arrangement which was to prove politically disastrous for the future.

The ruling families of England and France were closely related through a succession of marriage alliances. This strategy was particularly marked during the mid 13th century when Henry III of England and Louis IX of France, together with their respective younger brothers, Richard of Cornwall and Charles of Anjou, were all linked by their marriages to the four daughters of Raymond Berengar, the troubadour count of Provence, and his wife, Beatrix of Savoy. These family ties were extended when Henry's grandson, Edward II, married Isabella, the great-granddaughter of St Louis, in 1308. Such alliances were not confined to royalty (76).

St Louis had been renowned for his encouragement of the arts. Isabella's father, Philip IV, known as 'le Bel', was an equally generous and discriminating patron, particularly remembered for his link with the Parisian illuminator Honoré. Honoré's superb miniatures for 'La Somme le Roy' (77) joined the treasures of the British Library as recently as 1966, bequeathed by Dr Eric Millar, a former Keeper of Manuscripts, in memory of his mother. Specifically royal commissions among the finest English manuscripts are rarely identifiable but the Psalter of Prince Alphonso (80), generally regarded as the herald of the so-called East Anglian school of illumination, reveals its origins through its owner's arms, an increasingly popular decorative feature of manuscripts in which marginalia had assumed a major role. The science of heraldry was intensively developed during the 13th century, when major collections of coats-of-arms were variously compiled and circulated.

Detail from figure 103

Although the book of hours, introduced as a separate devotional manual during the mid 13th century (55), was very quickly adopted as a fashionable accessory in France and Flanders, it was never to achieve quite the same degree of success in England. There the elaborately decorated psalter continued to be the popular choice, its degree of richness offering a visual barometer of an owner's social status. During the 14th century many of the great psalters can be identified with their patrons through the inclusion of appropriate heraldry.

These patrons do not always represent the greatest or most famous families. The celebrated Luttrell Psalter (94) is an excellent example. Sir Geoffrey Luttrell was the owner of substantial estates in Lincolnshire and southern Yorkshire but enjoyed no very great public distinction. The decoration of his splendid book apparently reflects both his interests in his rural lifestyle and his pride in his family connections. His well-documented career was designed to enhance and consolidate the position of the family and its hold on its estates. The Luttrell sons and daughters contracted suitable marriages or entered local religious communities. Sir Geoffrey himself fulfilled the required military obligations of his class, summoned several times to serve in the Scottish border campaigns of Edward I and Edward II, but major historical events of the period seem largely to have passed him by. His eldest surviving son, Andrew, did however serve in France with Henry of Grosmont, Earl of Derby and afterwards Duke of Lancaster. Henry was esteemed throughout Europe as an embodiment of the chivalric ideal of the age, and was one of the original knights of the Order of the Garter, founded at Windsor by Edward III in 1348.

For the English upper classes, the last years of the 13th century and the first half of the 14th century offered much experience of knight service in the field both at home and abroad. Edward I (died 1307) campaigned in Wales and in Scotland and left a contrasting architectural heritage of massively defensive castles on the one hand, and the elegant and richly decorated memorial crosses marking the route of his beloved queen's cortege in 1290, on the other. Edward II continued to campaign in the north and was famously defeated by Robert the Bruce at Bannockburn in 1314. Deposed in 1327 after a number of years of very damaging civil strife, he was succeeded by his son, Edward III, whose reign saw the beginnings of the Hundred Years War with France. The death in 1328 of his maternal uncle, Charles IV of France, leaving no direct heir, gave the English king a potential claim to the French throne in the right of his mother, Isabella. His position as the French king's principal vassal through the Duchy of Aquitaine fuelled his ambitions. The war began in 1337 and its early years were marked by notable English victories at sea at Sluys (1340) and on land at Crécy (1346). It was spasmodically to dominate events on both sides of the Channel until the middle of the following century.

In southern Europe there were many political changes and realignments. The papal court removed from Rome to Avignon in the time of Pope

Clement V (1305–1314), a native of Gascony who elected to live on French soil, providing a new courtly focus for patronage of literature and the visual arts. The island kingdom of Sicily passed from French domination into the hands of the royal house of Aragon, introducing an important direct link between the Italian and Spanish peninsulas. On the mainland of southern Italy the kingdom of Naples continued to be ruled by the descendants of Charles of Anjou, whose grandson Robert the Wise (1309–1343) presided over a court which played a central role in the explosion of cultural achievement that took place in Italy during the first half of the 14th century (96), despite an unceasing background of political strife. Two outstanding painters left a legacy whose influence was to be felt far beyond their own land. The work of the Sienese artist Duccio (died 1318) was particularly reflected in book painting while Giotto (died 1337), who undertook commissions in several different parts of Italy, was characterised in the 16th century by the historian Vasari as having changed the language of painting from Greek to Roman.

In literature this was a golden age for Italian vernacular writing, producing within a single century three major authors whose names are still universally respected. Dante (1265–1321) composed his 'Divina Commedia' at the beginning of the century, setting its action on the Thursday before Easter in 1300. Its graphic verbal imagery was translated into visual form within a few decades of its author's death (109). Petrarch (1304–1374) was among those whose careers were influenced both by the papal court of Avignon, where he spent his early years, and by the patronage of Robert of Anjou. He received the laurel crown in 1341 and settled in Italy during the latter part of his life, leaving a reputation not only for his writings but also as a pioneer of the reintroduction of the lost master works of classical learning into European culture. Boccaccio (1313–1375) spent his formative years in Naples and followed Petrarch in the pursuit of classical learning. The work for which he is best known today, the collection of tales known as the 'Decameron', was compiled during the 1340s and made its first appearance in 1353.

The 'Decameron' is set in Florence against a background of the great plague, the Black Death, which swept through Europe just before the middle of the century. Huge numbers of people died and entire communities were wiped out by this natural disaster. In Italy its victims included Petrarch's beloved Laura (185) and two of the leading painters of the Sienese School, Ambrogio and Pietro Lorenzetti. In England, where it raged in 1348, the year of the foundation of the Order of the Garter, its impact upon the established economy and way of life of the country was incalculable.

2

Coment dieu done ses emandemes a moyses?

Comment typoenæ aourent le ueel.

77 (above)

76 (opposite)

Lives of Saints and other Devotional Pieces

St Eustace recalled from exile to serve his king

Northern France, beginning of the 14th century.
French; 235 x 175 mm, 232 fols.
Egerton MS 745, f.3b

The figure of a knight kneeling before the Virgin in one of the miniatures in this book wears the arms of the Counts of St Pol, who lived near Amiens. He was probably Guy de Châtillon (died 1317), whose wife Mary was a daughter of John Duke of Brittany and his wife, Princess Beatrice of England. Guy's own daughter Mary married Aymer de Valence, Earl of Pembroke, and was the foundress of Pembroke College in Cambridge. The relics of St Eustace were venerated in Paris and the St Pol family was closely associated with the French as well as the English court. The style of the best miniatures in this volume bears a family resemblance to the work of Honoré (77).

'La Somme le Roy'

Moses receiving the tablets of the law; the worship of the Golden Calf

France, Paris, end of the 13th century.
French; 185 x 120 mm, 208 fols.
Additional MS 54180, f.5b

The text of this book is a series of moral treatises compiled in 1279 for King Philip III of France (died 1285) by his confessor, the Dominican Frère Laurent. The work achieved great general popularity and was translated into several other languages. The 11 illustrations in this copy (plus two strays in the Fitzwilliam Museum in Cambridge) are the masterpieces of the Parisian miniaturist Honoré, one of the most significant figures in the history of Gothic painting. He lived and worked in Paris from at least 1288 to 1296 and seems to have been dead by 1318. King Philip IV of France was among his patrons.

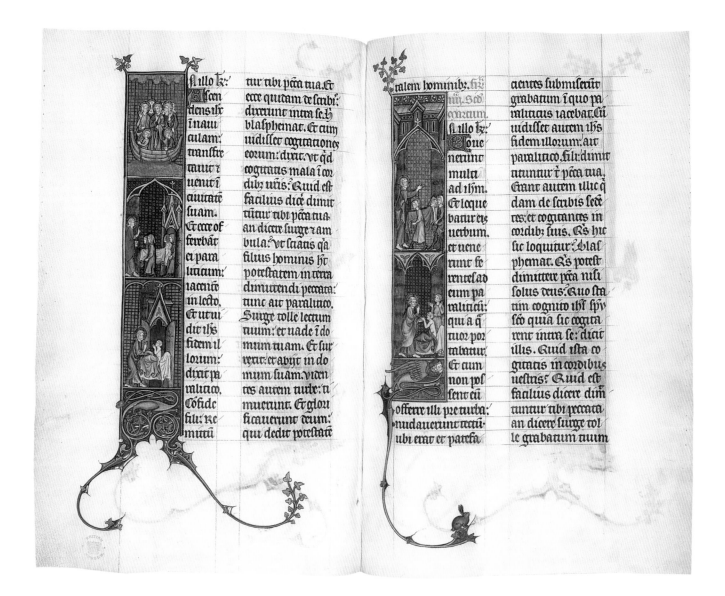

78

Gospel Lectionary

Christ performing miracles

France, Paris, end of the 13th century.
Latin; 310 x 200 mm, 173 fols.
Additional MS 17341, ff.123b–124

This manuscript is an exact copy of a lectionary made soon after the middle of the 13th century for the Sainte Chapelle in Paris, built by St Louis IX to house Christ's Crown of Thorns which he had acquired from the Latin emperor of Constantinople. It contains readings from the gospels for use at Mass during the liturgical year and almost all are illustrated, providing a complete sequence of scenes from the life of Christ. Some episodes, such as the miracles of healing seen here, are very rarely depicted. The style of the illumination is close to that of Honoré (77) and some of the work at the beginning of the manuscript may be attributable to him.

79

80

Scientific Treatises

Opening page of Ptolemy's 'Almagest': star-gazers; marginal animals with astronomical instruments

France, Paris, *c*.1300.
Latin; 410 x 290 mm, 560 fols.
Burney MS 275, f.390b

This very large and beautifully illuminated volume of scientific material, clearly intended from the first for high-ranking patrons, has a distinguished history. In 1387 Pope Clement VII gave it to John, Duke of Berry, one of the most famous book collectors of all time. Berry passed it on to his brother, the Duke of Orleans, but retrieved it after the latter's death in 1407. His arms are painted on its page edges and his secretary, Jean Flamel, added an ownership inscription at the beginning. The decoration of the book, fully worthy of Berry's discriminating taste, was carried out by one of the leading Parisian workshops of the last years of the 13th century.

Alphonso Psalter

Marginal subject of the battle between a knight and a griffin

England, London, *c*.1284.
Latin; 240 x 140 mm, 136 fols.
Additional MS 24686, f.18 (detail)

Usually regarded as the first major work of the 'East Anglian' period of English gothic illumination, this manuscript was begun to mark the projected marriage of Alphonso, heir apparent of King Edward I of England, to Margaret, daughter of Count Florens V of Holland. Alphonso died in 1284 before the marriage could take place and the book remained unfinished for some years. It was completed at the beginning of the 14th century, possibly for his sister Elizabeth (died 1316), who was married first to Count John I of Holland and then to Humphrey de Bohun, Earl of Hereford. The original decoration is of outstanding delicacy and realism, deriving stylistically from such 'court school' masterpieces as the Oscott Psalter (69) and the Westminster retable.

81 (above)

Psalter

The Nativity; the Crucifixion

Switzerland, diocese of Constance, c.1300.
Latin; 220 x 160 mm, 167 fols.
Additional MS 22280, ff.9b–10

The original owner of this manuscript, identified as 'Abt Rudolf', is portrayed in one of the four miniatures. The choice of saints commemorated in its calendar places it in the region of Constance. This area was originally a part of the great Germanic Empire but Switzerland, as it is constituted today, began to emerge in 1291 as a confederation of districts and towns united in their opposition to Habsburg domination. The book retains its original binding of wooden boards, covered with leather and fastened with brass clasps in the form of birds.

82 (opposite)

De Lisle Psalter

Scenes from the life of Christ

England, London or Westminster, c.1308 with later additions.
Latin and French; 340 x 225 mm, 19 fols (ff.117–135 of a composite volume).
Arundel MS 83 pt. II, f.124b

The text to which these magnificent illuminated leaves originally belonged has been completely lost. Only a calendar and a series of miniatures from the life of Christ and some theological diagrams are known. It is assumed from their scale and content that the book was a psalter, undoubtedly one of the grandest of the age, and it is known to have belonged to Sir Robert de Lisle (1288–1344), who gave it in 1339 to two of his daughters, nuns of the Gilbertine priory of Chicksands in Bedfordshire, of which the family were patrons. Sir Robert himself spent the last years of his life as a member of the Franciscan order. Several artists contributed to the manuscript. Its miniatures have a grandeur suggestive of painting on a larger scale than that of book decoration.

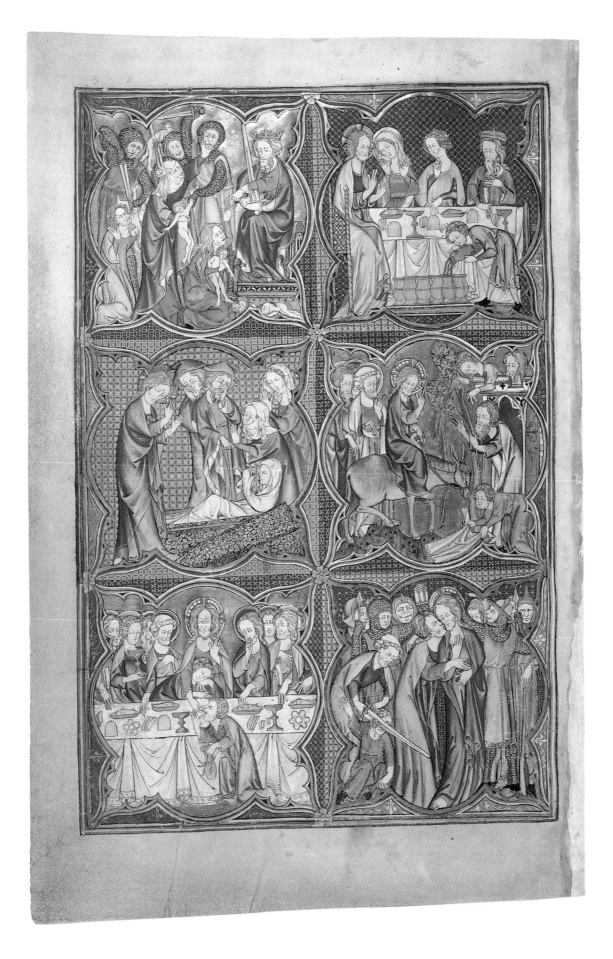

83 (above)

Antiphonal

The Resurrection

North-eastern France or Flanders, beginning of the
14th century.
Latin; 485 x 325 mm, single detached leaf.
Yates Thompson MS 25, f.1 (detail)

An antiphonal contains the chants to be sung during the
celebration of Mass. Very large-scale illuminated copies of this
music were often provided for use in major churches. They
would be placed on lecterns where they could be used by a
whole group of singers simultaneously. This detached leaf was
once part of an antiphonal made for a Dominican church
which has not been identified. It carries part of the music for
the feast of Easter.

84 (opposite)

Breviary of Marguerite de Bar (Winter portion)

The crucifixion of St Andrew; Christ calling the first of his disciples

Lorraine, *c*.1302–4.
Latin; 290 x 200 mm, 360 fols.
Yates Thompson MS 8, f.249b

This breviary, of which the summer portion is in the
Bibliothèque Municipale at Verdun, was commissioned by
Marguerite de Bar, abbess of St Maur at Verdun (died 1304).
It was made for her brother Renaud, provost of St Mary
Magdalen, Verdun in 1302 and bishop of Metz from 1302
until his death in 1316. Both are portrayed within the
manuscript and its decoration includes numerous examples of
their family coats of arms. A breviary contains all the material
necessary for the recitation of the eight services which make
up the daily office - matins, lauds, prime, terce, sext, none,
vespers and compline - which constitutes the routine pattern
of worship of the regular clergy. The lavish decoration of this
handsome book reflects French, English and Flemish work of
the period.

85 (above)

Apocalypse

The sounding of the first and second trumpets

Northern France, beginning of the 14th century.
Latin and French; 325 x 225 mm, 47 fols.
Additional MS 17333, ff.10b–11

The exact place of origin of this manuscript has not been established though Normandy has been suggested. A closely related copy is in the Metropolitan Museum of Art in New York. The Apocalypse was especially popular in England and it is possible that an English manuscript was the model from which this example was derived. The lack of depth in these miniatures and the monumentality of the principal figures have more in common with English than with Parisian painting of the time.

86 (opposite)

Bible

Tree of Jesse, with marginal scenes of the Annunciation, the Nativity and the Presentation

Northern Italy, possibly Venice, beginning of the 14th century.
Latin; 395 x 235 mm, 546 fols.
Additional MS 18720, f.410

The influence of Byzantine painting is very strong in the decoration of this fine bible. Venice, principal seaport in north-east Italy, had strong links with the eastern Mediterranean for many centuries, and similar influence is to be found in many of the buildings in the city. However, other work in this Byzantinising style can be linked with neighbouring Padua and the provenance of the bible, given its lack of supplementary evidence, is not certain, though its quality is beyond doubt. These subjects mark the beginning of St Matthew's Gospel.

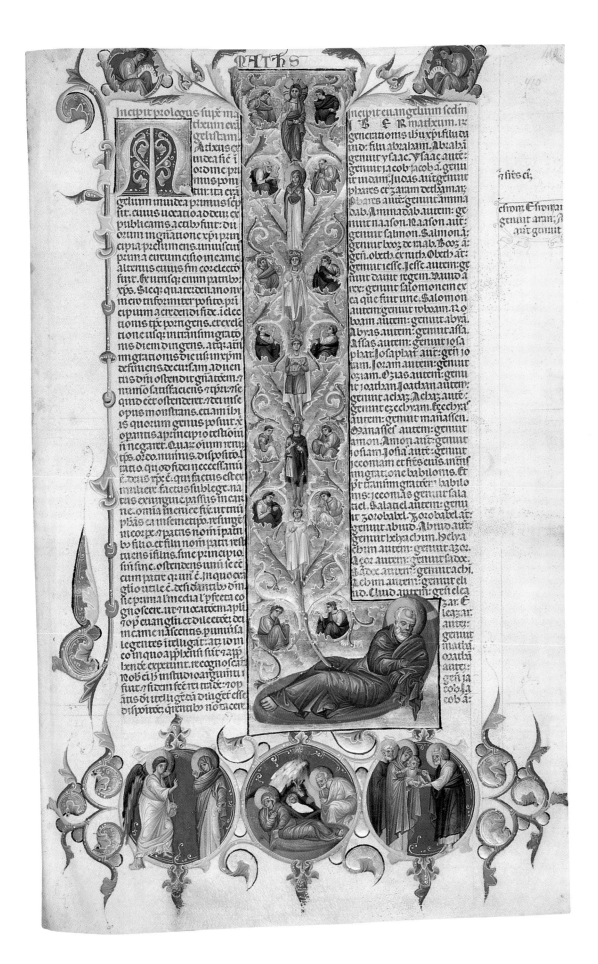

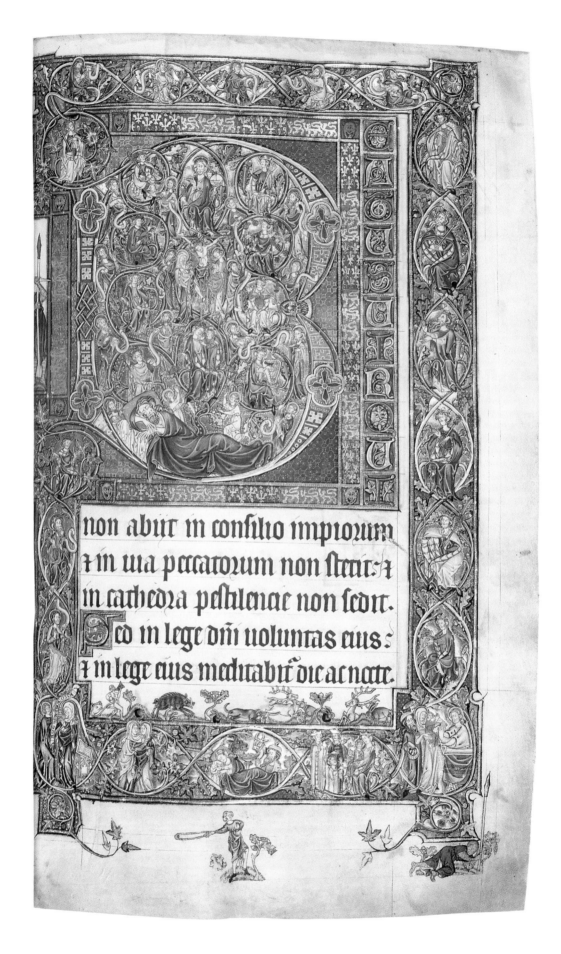

87 (opposite)

Gorleston Psalter

Beatus page with incidents and figures from the Old and New Testaments

England, East Anglian school, *c.*1310–20.
Latin; 375 x 235 mm, 228 fols.
Additional MS 49622, f.8

Made for an unidentified individual connected with the church of St Andrew at Gorleston in north-east Suffolk, this manuscript is one of the outstanding masterpieces of the so-called East Anglian school of illumination which flourished during the first quarter of the 14th century. The heraldry that forms an important element of its decoration suggests that it cannot have been made later than 1322. A full-page miniature of the crucifixion was added to it about 1325 but all the original illumination is confined to initials and margins. On this opening page of the psalms, scenes from the Christmas story, figures of David and Goliath, and a hunting sequence, are combined with figures of prophets, royal heraldry and a magnificent Tree of Jesse in a dazzling overall design.

88 (above)

Queen Mary's Psalter

David capturing Jerusalem and conquering the Philistines

England, probably London, *c.*1310–20.
Latin and French; 275 x 175 mm, 319 fols.
Royal MS 2 B. vii, f.56

One of the most lavishly illuminated manuscripts ever to be produced in England, this book contains about a thousand separate images, covering both Old and New Testaments, and including marginal cycles of scenes from the lives of saints, from the bestiary, and of different types of hunting. Its principal artist was equally at home working in gold and full colour and in delicately tinted outline drawing. There is no clue to the identity of the original owner though the scale of the commission has been thought to suggest a royal client. The book takes it name from the fact that it was given in the mid 16th century to Queen Mary Tudor. The scenes on this page reflect the military practices of the early 14th century.

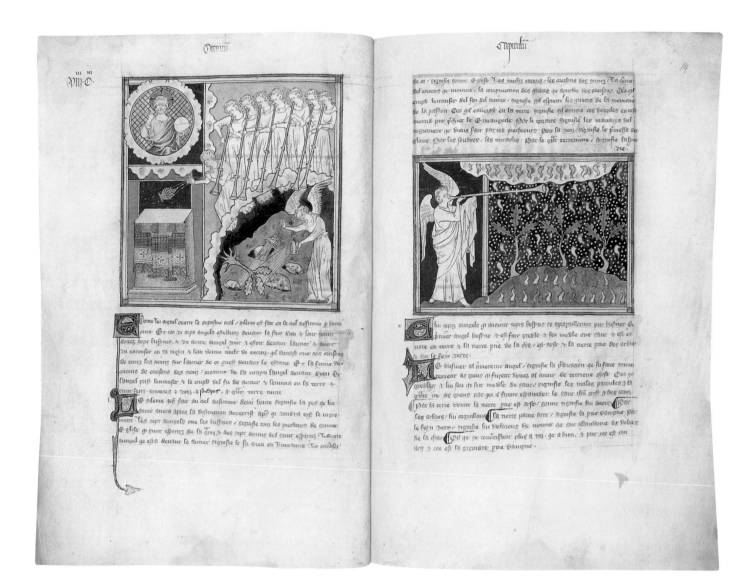

89 (opposite)

Legal Collection

Henry I; death of his sons in the White Ship

England, probably London, *c*.1321.
Latin; 320 x 210 mm, 133 fols.
Cotton MS Claudius D. ii, f.45b

Each section in this handsome legal compilation relating to the City of London, once part of a larger volume now also represented in the London Record Office and Oriel College, Oxford, is introduced by a figure of the king in whose reign the appropriate laws were promulgated. The miniatures were painted in the workshop responsible for Queen Mary's Psalter (88). The reign of King Henry I is additionally marked by a vignette of the wreck of the White Ship in which his two sons, William and Richard, perished, leaving his daughter Matilda as his sole heir and resulting in the civil wars of the mid 12th century. After this dreadful tragedy Henry is said never to have smiled again. The arms in the initial relate to Sir Robert Cotton and were added in the early 17th century.

90 (above)

Apocalypse

The angels with their trumpets and the censing of the altar; the sounding of the first trumpet

England, probably London, *c*.1310–25.
French; 305 x 210 mm, 45 fols.
Royal MS 19 B. xv, ff.13b–14

The unusual and distinctive decoration of this manuscript is due to three artists of the Queen Mary group, including the master himself (88). The miniatures are carried out in an effective combination of outline drawing and full colour, with the figures frequently standing out in unpainted vellum against a solid coloured ground. The graceful line of angels on the left-hand page represents English work of the period at its most delicate and courtly.

109

92 (above)

Breviary

David playing upon the bells

England, Norwich, 1322–25 and before 1383.
Latin; 290 x 205 mm, 295 fols.
Stowe MS 12, f.190 (detail)

The text of this breviary is of Sarum use, with the variations characteristic of the diocese of Norwich. Its date is indicated by a series of historical notes which include the execution of Thomas Earl of Lancaster in 1322 but omit the death of Bishop John Salmon of Norwich in 1325. Stylistically the book is closely related to the Gorleston Psalter (87), though its decoration is far less elaborate.

91 (above)

Pseudo-Aristotle: 'De Secretis Secretorum'

Aristotle and King Alexander exchanging letters

England, London, 1326–27.
Latin; 240 x 160 mm, 76 fols.
Additional MS 47680, f.10

This treatise was written out and presented to King Edward III by Walter de Milemete between October 1326 and March 1327, together with a sister manuscript, 'De nobilitatibus, sapientiis et prudentiis regum', which he had composed himself, and which is now at Christ Church, Oxford. Its lavish decoration, which is unfinished, was originally the work of four artists, added to at a later date by two further hands. Stylistically it is close to East Anglian work, especially to the Stowe Breviary (92).

93 (opposite)

St Omer Psalter

King David and his fool; scenes from the stories of Moses and Samson

England, East Anglian school, *c.*1325–30.
Latin; 330 x 220 mm, 175 fols.
Yates Thompson MS 14, f.57b

The original patrons of this manuscript were members of the St Omer family of Mulbarton in Norfolk, but it was not completed until it had passed into the hands of Humphrey, Duke of Gloucester (died 1447), younger brother of King Henry V, early in the 15th century. This is one of the original pages, featuring Old Testament scenes painted in minute detail and betraying the Italian influence which began to affect English book painting at about this time. The modelling of the figures, creating a very real feeling of volume, is particularly effective.

110

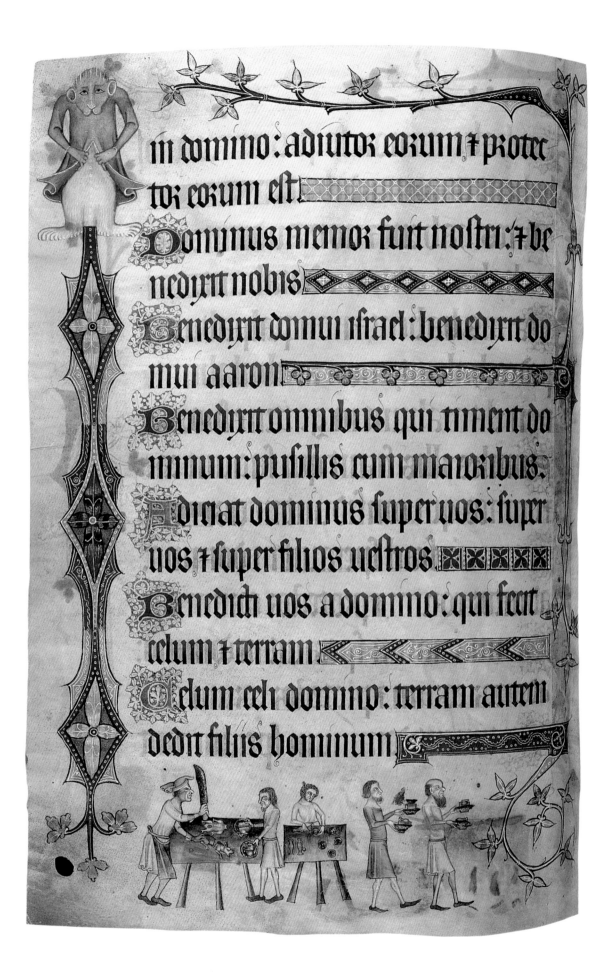

in domino: adiutor eorum + protec

tor eorum est

Dominus memor fuit nostri: + be

nedixit nobis

Benedixit domui israel: benedixit do

mui aaron

Benedixit omnibus qui timent do

minum: pusillis cum maioribus.

Adiciat dominus super vos: super

vos + super filios vestros

Benedicti vos a domino: qui fecit

celum + terram

Celum celi domino: terram autem

dedit filiis hominum

94 (opposite)

Luttrell Psalter

Preparations for a meal

England, diocese of Lincoln, *c*.1325–35.
Latin; 355 x 245 mm, 309 fols.
Additional MS 42130, f.207b

Famous as one of the richest of all sources for the illustration of contemporary everyday life in medieval England, this psalter was made for Sir Geoffrey Luttrell of Irnham in Lincolnshire (died 1345). Its illumination, though less polished than that of some of the slightly earlier manuscripts of the period, is of unsurpassed vitality and marks the last stage of the East Anglian style. No directly comparable work is known. The marginal scene, showing Sir Geoffrey's servants preparing to serve him at dinner, is one of a sequence of four, illustrating the work of his kitchens and ending with a depiction of the family and their guests at table.

95 (above)

Holkham Bible Picture Book

The Circumcision, the Journey of the Magi and the Flight into Egypt

England, possibly London, *c*.1320–30.
French; 285 x 210 mm, 42 fols.
Additional MS 47682, ff.13b–14

The Holkham Bible tells the story of man from the Creation to the Last Judgement. Each illustration is accompanied by a short explanatory text in Anglo-French. A significant number of apocryphal incidents are included and details are drawn from a variety of sources, not least the observation of contemporary everyday life. The book was apparently commissioned by a Dominican friar who is pictured saying to the artist: 'Now do it well and thoroughly, for it will be shown to important people.' It may thus have been designed as a teaching aid. It was acquired by the Library from the collection at Holkham Hall in Norfolk, hence its name.

poita fors desinoles paluz.
7 fors designes uoies. ales
totes uois por li vois hau
bal q. oil. qui auoit denát
mult mal ao. car per le
trauail 7 ple neiller 7 per
la uiolance de la froidure.
li couit il agrant dolor
fors de la teste. Mes ne que
dent pui ces malesauen

les romains metre deuerf
le lac. si qui ne poiffent en
nule ptie corner a foiltere
fee ne a garence. se il ne fe
metoient effort terres ou
il toft poroient les ines.
dont niot plus quant tat
aprode fe furent que des
lances 7 des espies aguz se
poient entre ferir. qui ne

---

96 (opposite)

Address of the City of Prato to Robert of Anjou

Robert of Anjou enthroned as King of Naples

Italy, Tuscany, 1335–40.
Latin; 480 x 340 mm, 30 fols.
Royal MS 6 E. ix, f.10b

The town of Prato in Tuscany had placed itself under the protection of Robert of Anjou and addressed itself to him in the Latin verse in this volume. Very large in format, it is illustrated with numerous finely painted miniatures mainly of a symbolical nature, including personifications of Italian cities such as Rome and Florence. Robert, who succeeded his father in 1309, was crowned at Avignon by Pope Clement V and became the recognised leader of the Guelph or papal party, opposing the Ghibellines who supported the emperor. He was the most powerful Italian prince of his day and also a man of learning, devoted to literature and a patron to Petrarch.

97 (above)

'Faits des Romans'

Hannibal and his elephants crossing the Alps

Italy, Naples, about 1340.
French; 330 x 230 mm, 363 fols.
Royal MS 20 D. i, f.275b (detail)

The 'Faits des Romains', drawn from a variety of sources, covers ancient history from Thebes in the time of Oedipus to Rome in the time of Pompey. Made in Naples towards the end of the reign of Robert of Anjou (96), this copy follows the Italian fashion of having its illustrations in the lower margins. Its artists were clearly fascinated by natural phenomena. In this miniature the winds are directing heavy blizzards of snow onto the heads of Hannibal and his troops as they toil across the mountains.

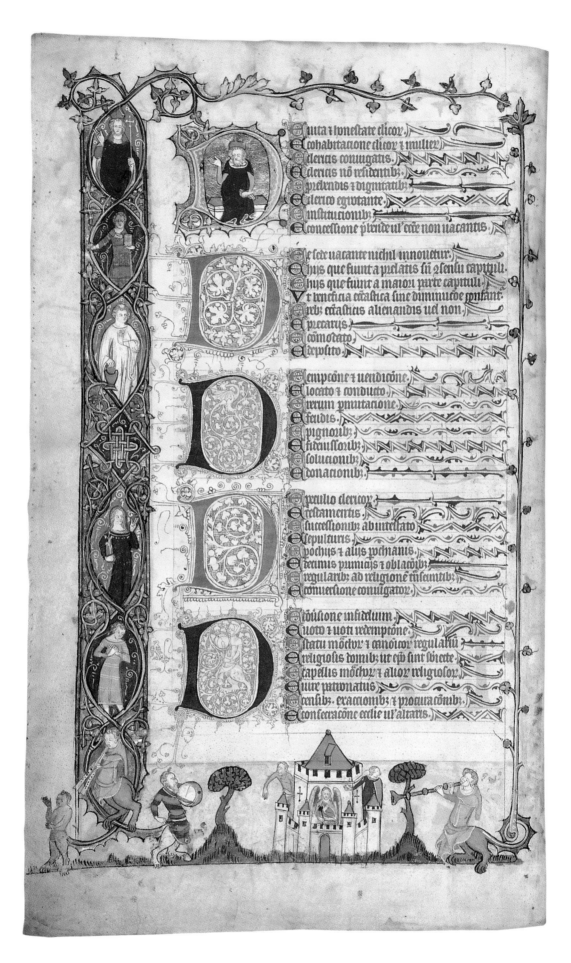

98 (opposite)

Smithfield Decretals

List of contents

England, probably London, *c*.1330–40.
Latin; 455 x 280 mm, 314 fols.
Royal MS 10 E. iv, f.2b

The main text of this massive volume of canon law is written
in a typically Italian script but its lavish decoration, including
more than 600 marginal subjects drawn from such varied
sources as the Bible, collections of miracle stories, animal
fables and chivalrous romances, was added in England. On
this particular page the script itself and the decorative
penwork initials are also English. In the late 15th century
the manuscript belonged to the Benedictine priory of
St Batholomew at Smithfield in London.

99 (above)

Book of Hours

The Emperor Titus besieging Jerusalem

England, perhaps London, *c*.1340–50.
Latin and French; 170 x 105 mm, 190 fols.
Egerton MS 2781, f.190

The book of hours, developed as a vehicle for private
devotion, contains eight short services in honour of the
Virgin Mary which follow, in simplified form, the eight divisions of the office in the breviary (84). It achieved great popularity from the mid 13th century and large numbers of
copies have survived. This example was made for an unidentified man and woman who are shown on several of its pages.
They must have been people of substance for the book is
elaborately decorated by a team of artists and contains about
100 miniatures which include a substantial number of apocryphal subjects. Two full-page miniatures of the siege of
Jerusalem, quite unrelated to the basic content of the manuscript, appear on the final leaf, offering graphic evidence of
the military practices of the 14th century.

117

100 (above)

Book of Hours

The Ascension; Pentecost

Italy, Treviso or Venice, mid 14th century.
Latin; 140 x 100 mm, 210 fols.
Additional MS 15265, ff.127b–128

Local saints included in the calendar of this manuscript
suggest a connection with Treviso, though it is likely that it
was ordered from a professional workshop in nearby Venice.
It is illustrated with an unusually long cycle of full-page
scenes from the life of Christ and the very strong influence of
Byzantine painting is immediately apparent. The tiny
inscription at the foot of each page gives an indication of the
intended subject for the guidance of the illuminator.

101 (opposite)

Sainte Chapelle Epistle Lectionary

The Holy Trinity; the Last Supper

France, Paris, *c.*1340–50.
Latin; 410 x 285 mm, 223 fols.
Yates Thompson MS 34, f.116b

This lectionary was made in Paris and almost immediately
adapted for the use of the Sainte Chapelle. It contains seven
historiated initials by an assistant of the celebrated illuminator
Jean Pucelle, active in Paris around 1320–1360, who played
an important role in the development of gothic painting in
northern Europe. He assimilated and transmitted influences
from Italy, particularly from Duccio and the Sienese school.
This assistant appears alongside Pucelle in the Billyng Bible,
now in the Bibliothèque nationale in Paris, and must
therefore be either Anciau de Cens or Jaquet Maci, both of
whom are named there.

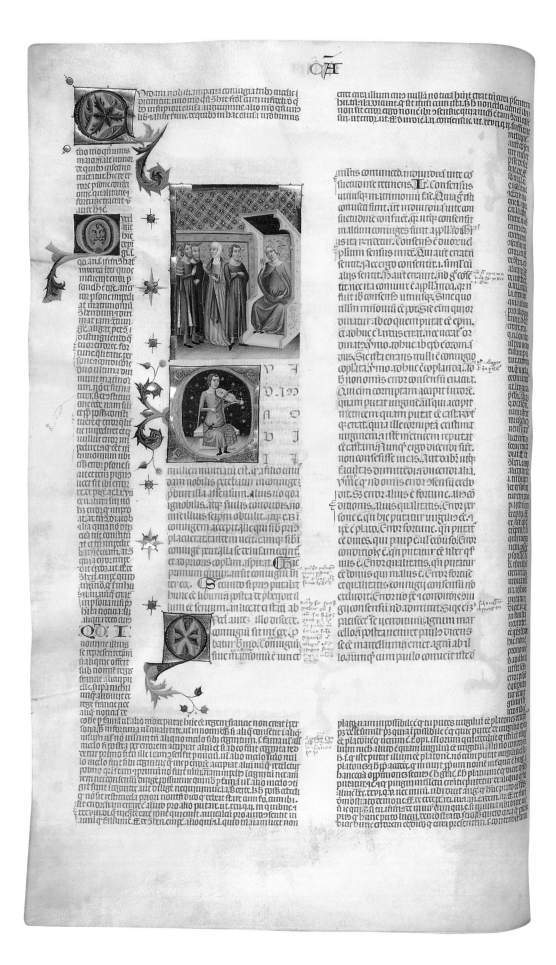

102 (opposite)

Gratian: 'Decretum'

Introductory miniatures to a chapter on marriage

Catalonia, Barcelona, mid 14th century.
Latin; 485 x 295 mm, 175 fols.
Additional MS 15275, f.82b

Gratian, a native of Tuscany, spent the greater part of his life
in the monastery of Sts Nabor and Felix in Bologna, where he
compiled his 'Concordia discordantium canonum', commonly
known as the 'Decretum', during the first half of the 12th
century. His work sets out to consolidate earlier collections of
canon law into a single coherent judicial system. It rapidly
gained universal acceptance among the universities and copies
circulated throughout Europe for the remainder of the
Middle Ages. Many of them are handsomely decorated. This
particular example, strongly influenced by Italian work of the
period, was produced by an illuminators' workshop in
Barcelona.

103 (above)

Helie de Borron: 'Meliadus'

A tournament

Italy, Naples, *c.*1352.
French; 340 x 230 mm, 352 fols.
Additional MS 12228, ff.215b–216

The 'Meliadus' is the first portion of the great medieval
romance of Palamedes, a part of the widely read and universally
popular Arthurian canon. This manuscript, which has 363
miniatures and drawings at the bottom of its pages, is associated
with Louis of Taranto, who married Queen Joanna of Naples,
granddaughter of Robert of Anjou (96) in 1347. He was styled
king by the pope in the following year, crowned in 1352, and
died a decade later. In many of the book's miniatures the hero,
Meliadus, father of Tristran, bears the Neapolitan arms.
Elsewhere in the volume there seem to be visual references to an
order of chivalry founded by Louis in 1352 in honour of the
Holy Ghost, the first such foundation in Italy.

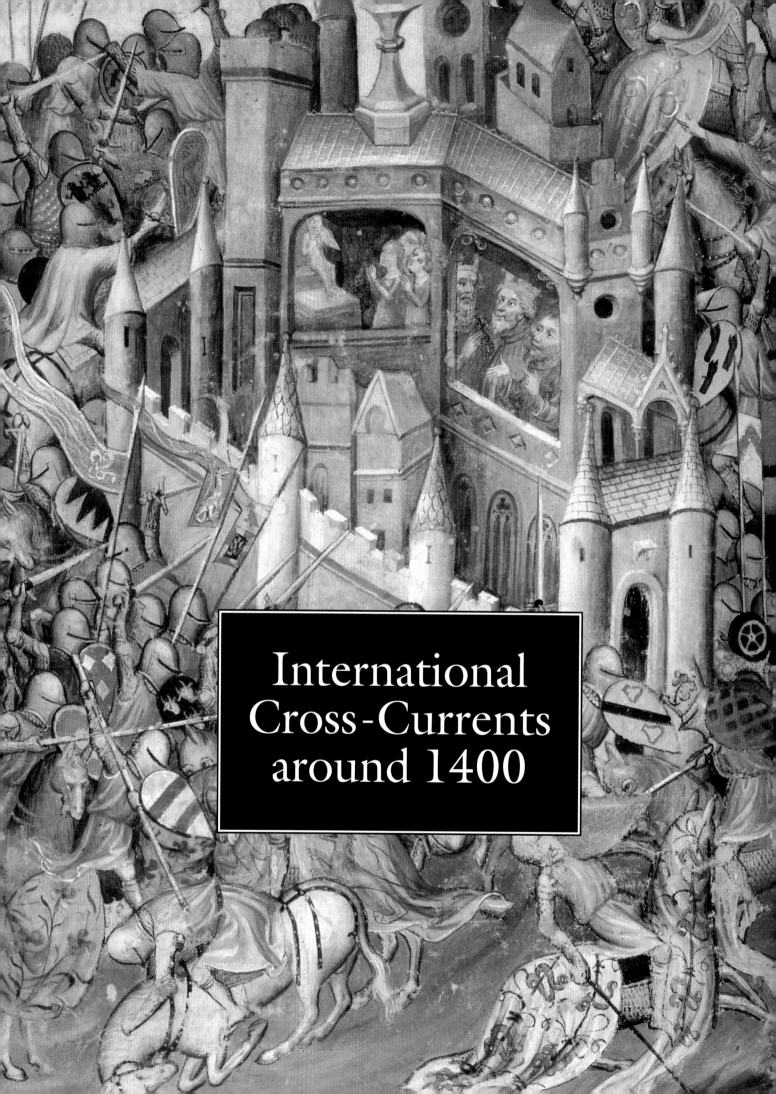

International
Cross-Currents
around 1400

The reputation of Paris as a centre for the illuminator's art was so strong and so well established that Dante could write in the 'Divina Commedia' as if the two were synonymous. This reputation was further enhanced during the second half of the 14th century under the patronage of King John the Good (died 1364) and his sons. King Charles V (died 1380) was particularly notable as the founder of the French royal library, for which many patristic and philosophical works previously available only in Latin were translated into French in versions that remained current for well over a century. He was also one of the first public figures to be consistently portrayed with lifelike and naturalistic features, reflecting a contemporary interest in the natural world (106). His brothers all shared an interest in art and culture. One of them, John, Duke of Berry (1340–1416), ranks among the greatest connoisseurs of all time and few men of any age have had a comparable influence on contemporary art (116). Louis, Duke of Anjou (died 1384) and Philip the Bold, Duke of Burgundy (died 1404) were similarly major patrons. This generation was also responsible for several dynastic and territorial links that were destined to prove very influential both politically and artistically. In 1384 Philip became Count of Flanders in the right of his wife Margaret, heiress of Louis de Mâle, initiating Burgundian interest in the southern Netherlands. Meanwhile Isabella of France (1348–1372), daughter of John the Good, had married Giangaleazzo Visconti (died 1402), Duke of Milan and the strongest of the contemporary rulers in northern Italy. The marriage of their daughter Valentina to Charles V's younger son Louis, Duke of Orleans, in 1389, brought to the French royal house an immediate and abiding interest in the affairs of northern Italy.

In England the final years of Edward III's reign produced such fine examples of book painting as the Egerton Genesis (104) and the devotional books of the Bohun family (108), both betraying an awareness of Italian art. Edward's immediate heir, Edward the Black Prince, victor of Poitiers (1356) and universally admired as the very embodiment of chivalry, predeceased his father in 1376. When the old king died in 1377 he was therefore succeeded by his grandson, Richard II, born in 1367 in Bordeaux where he spent his infancy. Politically Richard's reign was not a happy period, marred by the Peasants' Revolt (1381), the king's assumption of absolute power and his eventual defeat and deposition in 1399, to be replaced by his cousin Henry of Lancaster as King Henry IV. Artistically it was, however, a notable period, marked by such masterpieces as the Wilton Diptych, the great royal hall at Westminster, and the remarkable series of royal tomb figures commemorating Edward III, the Black Prince, Richard II himself and his first wife, Anne of Bohemia. Richard's marriage in 1383 to Anne, daughter of the Emperor Charles IV, established important political and artistic links with the German

Detail from figure 121

empire. Her death in 1394, which seems quite genuinely to have devastated Richard, freed him to cement a new alliance with France. In 1396 he married Isabella of France, the infant daughter of King Charles VI. England also acquired strong and lasting links with Spain and Portugal through the marriage of the king's uncle, John of Gaunt, Duke of Lancaster (died 1399), to Constance, heiress of Castile, and the alliances of two of his daughters with kings of Portugal and Castile.

France also suffered a royal minority. Charles VI was only twelve when he succeeded his father in 1380. He too, in 1385, contracted a marriage which brought links with Germany, taking as his queen Isabeau of Bavaria, in a three-way alliance which also saw Margaret of Bavaria married to John the Fearless, heir of Philip of Burgundy (135), and William of Bavaria, afterwards Count of Holland, to John's sister Margaret of Burgundy. In 1392 Charles suffered an attack of madness, resulting in a dramatic power struggle between other members of the royal family, culminating in the assassination of his brother, Louis of Orleans, in 1407, at the instigation of his cousin, John of Burgundy.

Despite these political upsets, the appetite for illuminated manuscripts remained undiminished on both sides of the Channel. English work of the time is marked by a number of large-scale books intended for use in public worship. Represented here by the Lovel Lectionary (123) and the Wyndham Payne Crucifixion (122), but also including Abbot Litlyngton's Missal at Westminster Abbey and the magnificent Sherborne Missal owned by the Duke of Northumberland, some of these manuscripts are on a scale that rivals the great bibles of the Romanesque period. In their own time they may be compared with the monster choirbooks produced to adorn the churches of Italy (110, 114). Close ties with the Netherlands, which supplied both artists (124) and manuscripts (125) for the English market, are also apparent around 1400. French work, both devotional and secular, is characterised by the recognisable input of schools of both the Netherlands and Italy (117, 121, 127, 128, 134, 135). The patronage of John of Berry is known to have embraced artists from both these regions, attracted into his personal service and extending their influence beyond its confines (127, 135).

The range and variety of Italian manuscripts is remarkable. Their narrative cycles embrace both religious (113) and secular (109) themes, while their large-scale miniatures (110) place them near to panel and monumental painting. Their sharp observation of nature and of contemporary life (115) brings the whole period very close to us.

In literary terms the late 14th century was also a notable age. Petrarch and Boccaccio both lived well into the second half of the century. Petrarch (died 1374) was among the first men of letters to attract the patronage of the various noble houses of Italy, including the Visconti in Milan, the Gonzaga of Mantua, the Este at Ferrara and the Malatesta in Rimini. He served variously as diplomat and orator, continued his studies of the classical past, maintained a close friendship with Boccaccio and eventually died among his books on the eve of his seventieth birthday. Boccaccio (died 1375) turned in his later years from fiction to topography, history and classical mythology and from Italian to Latin. It was on these later works, and in particular on 'De casibus virorum illustrium', which deals with the lives of famous men fallen from happiness and high estate into misery, that his reputation rested until well into the 16th century. 'De casibus' was translated into French in 1400 by Laurent de Premierfait, and many times reproduced in luxurious illuminated copies for discerning bibliophiles.

In France the major literary figure was the poet Guillaume de Machaut (died 1377), a canon of the cathedral of Reims, who enjoyed great renown within his own lifetime. In England Langland's *Vision of Piers Plowman* appeared in three distinct forms between 1367 and 1387 and the English translation of the bible associated with the name of John Wycliffe (died 1384) was made. The greatest English name of the period was of course that of Geoffrey Chaucer, whose career reflects the experiences and opportunities which might be available to a man of culture in the second half of the 14th century. Born about 1340 into a family of London vintners, he was educated as a page in the household of the Duchess of Clarence, wife of Edward III's second son, served briefly in the French wars in 1359, and was taken prisoner. He attracted the patronage of the king's third son, John of Gaunt, whose long-term mistress and eventual third wife, Katherine Swynford, was the poet's sister-in-law. He undertook trade and diplomatic missions for both Edward and his successor, visiting Italy on more than one occasion, and was later clerk of the works at various royal palaces. His immortal *Canterbury Tales*, among his later works, reflects his acquaintance with French and Italian literature, his observation of the different classes of society he had encountered in contemporary England, and the major social phenomenon of the pilgrimage to Becket's shrine, so prominent a feature of the county of Kent in which he lived. He died in 1400, and it is sad that no illuminator ever devised a pictorial cycle to accompany his lively narrative.

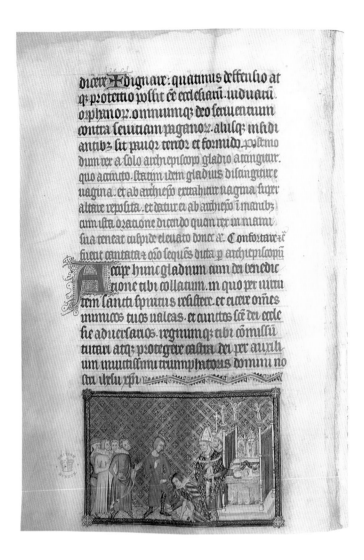

105 (above)

Guyart des Moulins: 'La Bible Historiale'

Elijah carried up to heaven in a fiery chariot

France, Paris, 1357.
French; 395 x 285 mm, 264 fols.
Royal MS 17 E, vii (pt. 1), f.166b (detail)

The 'Bible Historiale' enjoyed great popularity during the later Middle Ages and was frequently copied. Compiled between 1291 and 1294, it consists of a translation into French of the text of the bible, interspersed with passages from the 'Historia Ecclesiastic' of Petrus Comestor. This example is decorated in a fashionable and restrained semi-grisaille, heightened with colour and gold.

104 (opposite)

Egerton Genesis

The exit from Noah's Ark

England, third quarter of the 14th century.
French; 245 x 195 mm, 20 fols.
Egerton MS 1894, f.4

This manuscript consists of 20 leaves of illustrations to the first book of the Old Testament, executed in an idiosyncratic style strongly influenced by Italian work of the age of Giotto and Duccio. Style and iconography reflect an awareness of late Antique traditions. Essentially a picture book with a commentary rather than an illustrated text, it includes passages taken from the 'Historia Scholastical' of Petrus Comestor'.

106 (above)

Coronation Book of Charles V of France

The king invested with his spurs; the king placing his sword on the altar

France, Paris, 1365.
Latin; 280 x 190 mm, 108 fols.
Cotton MS Tiberius B. viii, f.48b

Charles V of France succeeded to the throne in 1364 when his father, John the Good, captured by the English at the Battle of Poitiers, died after spending most of the rest of his life as a prisoner in England. He commissioned an illustrated record of his coronation in which he is recognisably portrayed in many of the miniatures. He is thus one of the earliest historical figures whose true likeness has come down to us. Charles was also one of the first serious collectors of secular books, amassing a library of some 900 volumes which laid the foundations for the national library of France.

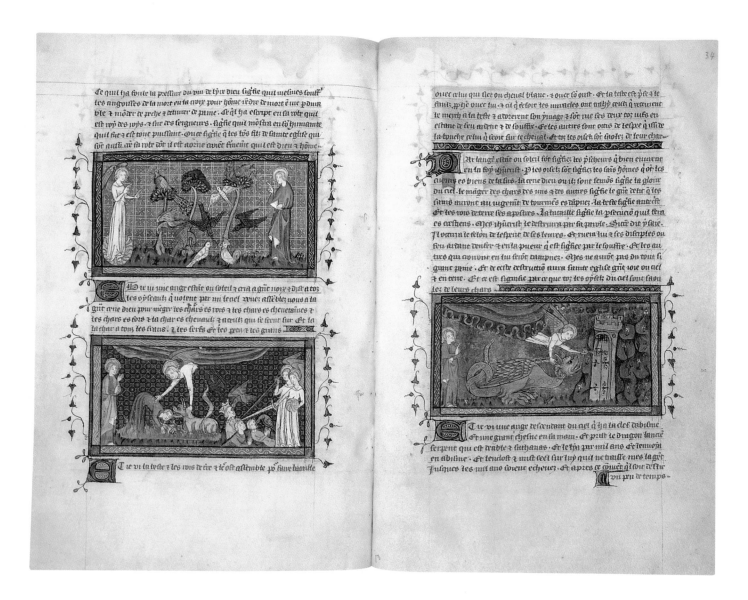

107 (above)

Apocalypse

The summoning of the fowls; the beast and the false prophet; the dragon imprisoned

France, Paris, third quarter of the 14th century.
French; 265 x 180 mm, 40 fols.
Yates Thompson MS 10, ff. 33b–34

At first sight much less elegant and sophisticated than some of the Apocalypse manuscripts made earlier in the century, this lively little book in fact has a good deal in common with the Coronation Book of Charles V (106), at least as far as its figure style is concerned. The artist takes delight in lively narrative, especially when portraying beasts and dragons, and his birds are naturalistically represented.

La busera infernal che mai non resta.
mena li spirti cola sua rapina.
uoltando e percotendo li molesta.
Quando giungon dinanzi ala ruina.
quiui li strida el compianto lamento.
bestemian quini la uirtu diuina.
Intesi chai cosi fatto tormento.
enno dannati i peccator carnali.
che la raggion somettreno al talento.
E come gli stornei ne portan lali.
nel freddo tempo a schiera larga e piena.
chosi quel fiato li spirti mali.

108 (opposite, below)

Bohun Psalter and Hours

The Three Maries at Christ's tomb; they take the news of the Resurrection to his disciples

South-east England, probably Pleshey, *c*.1361–73.
Latin; 395 x 230mm, 170 fols.
Egerton MS 3277, f.142 (detail)

The Bohun family, earls of Hereford, are renowned for a succession of splendidly illuminated devotional books made for them during the second half of the 14th century. Much of the work is in a very distinctive style and the family are known to have employed an Augustinian friar named John de Teye as a personal illuminator at their castle at Pleshey in Essex. This manuscript was apparently begun for a Humphrey de Bohun, possibly the 6th Earl (died 1361) but more probably the 7th Earl (died 1373), who was the grandfather of King Henry V through his daughter Mary (died 1394). In the margin to the left of the historiated initial B are scenes of several episodes in the funeral ceremonies of a knight. His effigy lies on a carved tomb, adorned with the arms of Fitzalan, earls of Arundel, who several times intermarried with the Bohuns.

109 (above)

Dante Alighieri: 'Divina Commedia'

Scenes from the Inferno: Minos judging; the condemnation of the carnal sinners; Dante in a faint

Italy, Naples, *c*.1370.
Italian; 310 x 240 mm, 178 fols.
Additional MS 19587, f.8 (detail)

Dante's celebrated poem was already attracting extensive cycles of illustration within a short time of the author's death in 1321. The 'Inferno', with its frequent references to historical and literary characters, proved particularly attractive to illuminators. The greatest of all Italian poets, Dante was born in Florence in 1265. Throughout his life he was active in local politics and his support for the Guelph faction led eventually to exile from his native city, to which he never returned after 1309. The *Divine Comedy*, composed during the later years of his life, was the greatest of his many writings. He is also celebrated for his life-long romantic devotion to Beatrice Portinari, which was not diminished by her death in 1290.

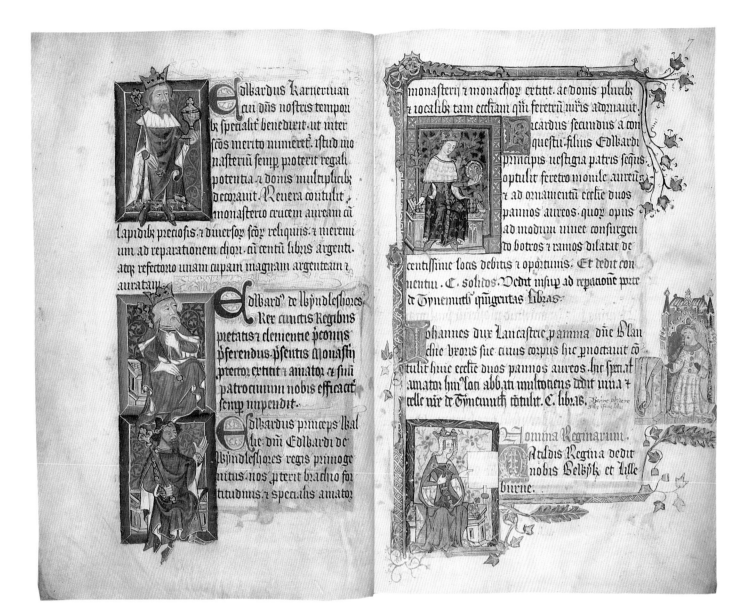

110 (opposite)

Gradual of Santa Maria degli Angeli

The Annunciation

Italy, Florence, *c.*1375.
Latin; 340 x 290 mm, detached cutting.
Additional MS 35254 C

This very large initial R is cut from a choirbook of enormous proportions containing music required during the celebration of Mass. The book was made for the Camaldolese monastery of Santa Maria degli Angeli in Florence. This miniature is attributable to Don Silvestro dei Gherarducci, a monk of the house, who had joined the order in 1348 when he was aged only nine. He was a famed painter and miniaturist and his work is praised by Vasari. Many other cuttings are known, stolen during the Napoleonic period. The remaining portion of the manuscript is now in the Laurentian Library in Florence.

111 (above)

The Golden Book of St Albans

Royal benefactors: Edward II, Edward III, the Black Prince, Richard II, John of Gaunt and Queen Matilda

England, St Albans, 1380 with later additions.
Latin; 365 x 230 mm, 157 fols.
Cotton MS Nero D. vii, ff.6b–7

Abbot Thomas de la Mare (1350–96) ordered this impressive record of the names of benefactors of St Albans, with details of their individual gifts to his community. It was compiled by a St Albans monk and historian, Thomas Walsingham, and written out by another member of the house, William de Wyllum. Illustrations were provided by a lay illuminator called Alan Strayler, who included his own portrait, having donated materials and given his time for the project.

Como Jabin Re de Assor aldando la destrucione che aveua fato Josue de Cotante cita e la otisione de tanti Re e de cotanto milia ponolo de quelle Cita e la grande crudelta per paura chel no fosse fato a ello e a la soa prouincia el mando Ambassaore a Jobab re de Moon e al Re de Semeron al Re de Acsach e a tuti li Re de aquilon li quale habitaua ale montagne e ala pianura e contra elmego di in la terra de Ceneroth e ali Re de

la pianura e dela region de Dor apresso elmare e ali Re deli Cananei che staua in oriente e in occidente e deli Amorei e deli Etei e deli Ferezei e deli Jebusei che staua ala montagna e deli Euei che habitaua ale rai re del monte de Hermon in la prouincia de Masphe che tuti questi Re cum tuta la soa gente uegnisse e fosse de compagnia cu ello a defenderse da Josue e dal ponolo de israel alamorte e ala destrucion de Josue e del ponolo de israel. Como li ambassaore de Jabin Re de Assor fe la soa Ambassa a tuti li Re sourascriti e tuti fo molto contenti de fare ogni cossa che consena el Re Jabin per defension de quilli piece.

Como vintiquatro Re de le sourascrite terre uene cascuno cu la soa gente da pe e da caualo homini da arme che segondo el maustro dele ystorie scholastiche fo trecento milia homini da arme e da milia carri. E segondo la bibia in lo libro de Josue al undecimo capitolo. Egressi qz sunt omnes cum turmis suis populus multus nimis sicut arena que est in littore maris. Equitatus et curus in mense multitudinis conuenerut qz omnes reges isti inuicem ro aquas meron ut pugnarent contra israel etcetera. Li enh tuti coe tuti li sourascriti Re cum le sor gente tropo gran ponolo segondo che si e elsabion inlo lio del mare. Chaualaria e charri de tropo grande multitudine. E tuti questi Re se conuene in una cossa ale aque de meron per combatere contra el ponolo de israel.

114

Fragment of a Choirbook Initial

The execution of St John the Baptist

Italy, Bologna, late 14th century.
Latin; 210 x 140 mm (entire cutting), single detached
fragment.
Additional MS 71119 D

The manuscript to which this fragment originally belonged
was a large volume of liturgical music illuminated by, or
within the immediate circle of, Niccolò di Giacomo di
Nascimbene, usually known as Niccolò da Bologna, who was
born about 1330 and died shortly after 1400. He was one of
the most successful illuminators of his day and his career can
be followed in some detail because, unusually at so early a
date, he made a habit of signing and dating much of his
work. In the late 1380s he was official illuminator to the cor-
poration of Bologna. This manuscript must have been closely
related to an impressive group of eight large choirbooks, now
in the Biblioteca Estense in Modena, which were designed for
the abbey of St Michele in Bosco, just outside Bologna.

112 (previous pages, left)

'Breviari d'Amor'

The fall of the rebel angels; devils at work

Catalonia, last quarter of the 14th century.
Catalan; 360 x 240 mm, 259 fols.
Yates Thompson MS 31, f. 43

The 'Breviari d'Amor', originally a Provençal poem composed
between 1288 and 1292 by Matré Ermengau of Béziers,
appears here in a Catalan prose translation. The work is an
encyclopaedic compilation in which theology and religious
history are juxtaposed with precepts on love from the works
of the troubadours. It explains how the world is an emanation
of love. This manuscript, the finest of five known copies in
Catalan, includes numerous miniatures in a style heavily
influenced by Italian work from Siena and Bologna.

113 (previous pages, right)

Old Testament Picture Book

Scenes from the Book of Joshua

Northern Italy, probably Padua, late 14th century.
Italian; 330 x 235 mm, 86 fols.
Additional MS 15277, f.73

The illustrations in this volume cover the books of the Old
Testament from Exodus to Joshua. A manuscript containing
complementary pictures for Genesis and Ruth is in the
Biblioteca dell' Accademia dei Concordi at Rovigo in
north-east Italy, about 25 miles south of Padua where the
book is thought to have been made. Its style has been
compared to monumental painting of the period and, in
particular, to the work of Jacopo da Verona. The illuminator
excels in portraying both spatial depth and movement. The
picture of an army on the march is particularly striking.

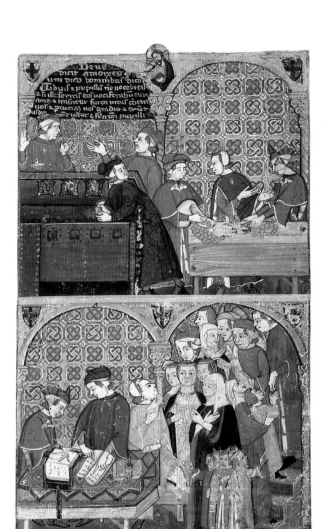

115 (above, left and right)

Treatise on the Vices

Banking and usury; plant and insect decoration

Italy, Genoa, late 14th century.
Latin; 175 x 115 mm, 15 fols and 7 fols.
Additional MS 27695, f. 8 (left);
Additional MS 28841, f. 5b (right).

These leaves come from two of the surviving fragments of a treatise on the vices, accompanied by a collection of incidents from the history of Sicily in the time of Frederick II (1298–1337), composed by a member of the Cocharelli family of Genoa for the instruction of his children. Many of its anecdotes came down to him from his grandfather, Pelegrino Cocharelli. Historical references suggest that the two treatises were written before 1324. Several of the book's miniatures escaped the destruction of the volume and they include particularly graphic scenes of contemporary Italian life. The decoration of the text pages is frequently inspired by nature and its accuracy suggests personal study of the subjects portrayed.

116 (overleaf, left)

Honoré Bonet (or Bouvet): 'Larbre des Batailles'

Introductory diagram representing contemporary rulers

France, c.1400.
French; 395 x 275 mm, 165 fols.
Royal MS 20 C. viii, f.2b

Written by Honoré Bonet, prior of Selonnet in Provence and afterwards abbot of L'Île-Barbe, 'Larbre des Batailles' was dedicated to King Charles VI of France. This particular copy at one time belonged to the king's bibliophile brother, John, Duke of Berry. It is unusual in containing the splendid frontispiece, mentioned in the author's dedicatory letter, which depicts pairs of contemporary rulers, identified by banners bearing the appropriate coats of arms. At the top of the tree stands Fortune with her wheel and at its foot we are shown the discords of the common people.

117 (above)

Book of Hours

Calendar page for August: the zodiac sign Virgo; a cooper at work

Italy, Bologna, end of the 14th century.
Latin; 130 x 100 mm, 189 fols.
Additional MS 34247, f.8

The illumination in this attractive little manuscript is the work of an artist whose style descends from that of Niccolò da Bologna (114). It reappears in France about 1400 in manuscripts made for John, Duke of Berry, where the style is associated with an artist known as the Master of the Brussels Initials. Whether or not the two artists are identical remains open to question. This book is quite clearly a product of Italy and its content suggests a link with the Augustinian monastery of San Salvatore in Bologna.

118 (above)

'Grandes Chroniques de France'

Angels prepare to carry St Louis IX up to heaven

France, Paris, *c.*1400.
French; 405 x 285 mm, 163 fols.
Sloane MS 2433 C, f. 7b (detail)

Composed at the end of the 14th century, the 'Grandes Chroniques' covers the history of France from its beginnings to the early part of the reign of Charles VI, who succeeded to the throne in 1380 at the age of twelve. The book rapidly became very popular and numerous illustrated copies were quickly made, many of them involving work by the leading illuminators of the day. This restrained and delicately painted miniature of St Louis on his deathbed is closely related to the much more elaborate and colourful composition depicting the Siege of Troy (121).

119 (opposite)

120 (above)

'Le Canarien'

The expedition to the Canary Islands at sea

France, Paris, after 1404.
French; 270 x 180 mm, 36 fols.
Egerton MS 2709, f.2

An expedition to the Canary Islands, described in this
contemporary account by two of its chaplains, was
undertaken in 1402–4 by two French knights named Gadifer
de la Sale and Jehan de Béthencourt. The islands are situated
in the Atlantic, about 60 miles off the African coast. Sailing
from La Rochelle, the expedition landed on Lanzarote in July
1402. La Sale remained to conquer and explore the individual
islands while Béthencourt sailed to Cadiz for reinforcements,
returning with the title of king bestowed upon him by Henry
III of Castile. The two men understandably fell out and La
Sale returned to France. This miniature of the expedition
under sail is the work of an anonymous illuminator known as
the Master of the Cité des Dames, from his work on copies of
Christine de Pisan's poem of that name.

'Biblia Pauperum'

Doubting Thomas testing the wound in Christ's side, flanked by Gideon's sacrifice and Jacob wrestling with the angel

Holland, The Hague, c.1395–1400.
Latin; 175 x 380 mm, 31 fols.
King's MS 5, f.25

In the 'Biblia Pauperum' a sequence of miniatures of scenes
from the life of Christ is accompanied by Old Testament
subjects regarded as their prefigurations. The work originated
in Germany and almost all the copies were made there. This
exceptionally beautiful Dutch example is unique both in
provenance and in quality. Written out luxuriously in red,
blue and gold and illustrated by the outstanding Dutch
miniaturist of the period, it was probably made for a member
of the court at The Hague, perhaps Albrecht, Duke of
Bavaria and Count of Holland (died 1404) or his second
wife, Margaret of Cleves.

121 (opposite)

'Les Livres des Histoires'

The siege of Troy

France, Paris, beginning of the 15th century.
French; 375 x 270 mm, 414 fols.
Stowe MS 54, f.185b

Painted probably in Paris but by a Flemish-born artist
inspired by a Neapolitan model, this action-packed miniature
exemplifies the international cross-fertilisation of the arts in
the period around 1400. It is one of the illustrations to a
universal history covering many of the most famous episodes
from Antiquity, from the birth of Oedipus to the campaigns
of Pompey, including the stories of Jason and the Golden
Fleece, the siege and ultimate capture of Troy, and the
exploits of Aeneas. The Greek and Trojan forces described by
Homer appear here in the guise of knights of the age of
European chivalry and romance.

122 (above)

Wyndham Payne Crucifixion

England, probably London, *c.*1405–1410.
No text; 375 x 260 mm, detached leaf.
Additional MS 58078

Originally intended to face the canon, or prayer of consecra-
tion, in a large missal, this detached miniature is one of
the great works of art of its period. It takes its name from
a former owner, Mr A. Wyndham Payne of Sidmouth in
Devon, who bought it in a Cirencester antique shop believing
it to be a reproduction. Although it is quite badly faded from
long exposure to daylight, the quality of the modelling,
particularly of the body of Christ, remains outstanding.
The miniature has been associated with the name Herman
Scheerre, an illuminator who probably originated in the
Lower Rhineland but who spent most of his working life in
England. Recent opinion suggests that it may rather be
related to one of the several hands in the 'Big' Bible (133).

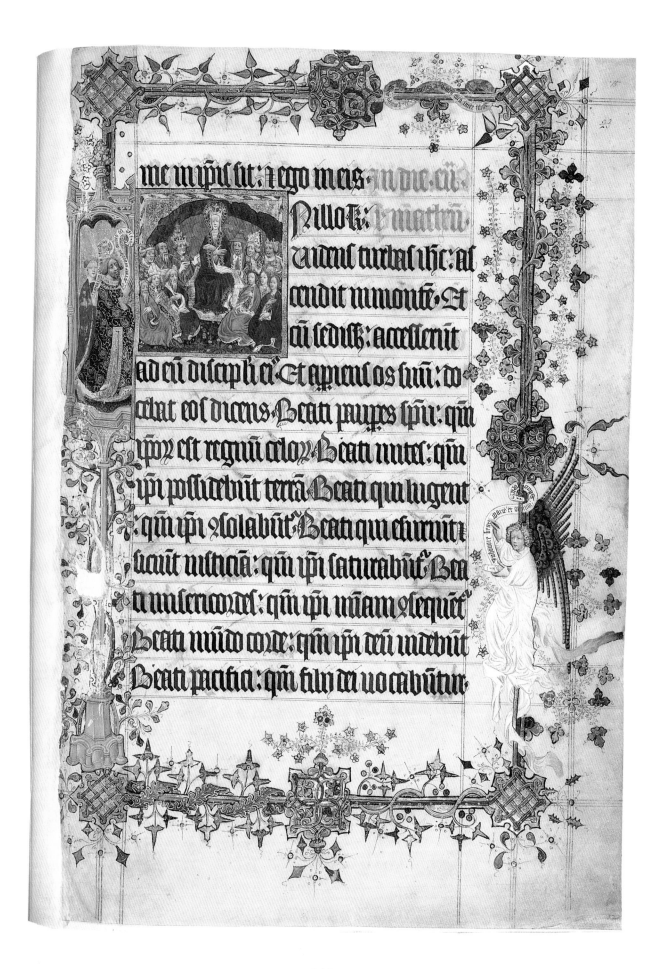

123 (opposite)

Lovel Lectionary

The Virgin Mary enthroned among the saints

England, diocese of Salisbury, before 1408.
Latin; 470 x 310 mm, 22 fols.
Harley MS 7026, f.15

Only a few disconnected leaves remain from what must once have been an exceptionally grand gospel lectionary commissioned by John Lord Lovel of Titchmarsh (died 1408) for use in Salisbury cathedral, probably during the time of Bishop Richard Mitford. Lovel intended that it should serve as a permanent memorial to him and to his wife Maud, both of whom are seen in the margin beside the miniature. Maud was the heiress of Robert Lord Holland and her great-uncle Thomas had been the first husband of Princess Joan of Kent, mother of Richard II by her subsequent marriage to the Black Prince. The Lovels were thus on the fringes of the royal kindred. The principal artist of this manuscript was the Dominican friar John Siferwas, famed for his work on the great missal of Sherborne Abbey in Dorset, which was also produced in Bishop Mitford's time.

124 (above)

Beaufort Hours

St Christopher

England or the Southern Netherlands, perhaps after 1401.
Latin; 215 x 150 mm, one of a series of 12 insertions into a manuscript of 240 fols.
Royal MS 2 A. xviii, f.11b

This lovely miniature of the patron saint of travellers is one of 12 early 15th-century miniatures which now form part of a mid-15th-century book of hours, once owned by Margaret Beauchamp, Duchess of Somerset, mother of Lady Margaret Beaufort and grandmother of King Henry VII. Further miniatures from the same series remain in an early 15th-century psalter now in Rennes. Among the subjects is the Yorkshire saint John of Bridlington (died 1379), who was canonised in 1401. The artist worked extensively for English patrons but was in fact a native of the southern Netherlands. He takes his name, the Master of the Beaufort Saints, from this manuscript.

125 (above)

Book of Hours

The Nativity

Southern Netherlands, Bruges, early 15th century.
Latin; 195 x 150 mm, 156 fols.
Additional MS 18213, f.34 (detail)

This is one of the many books of hours made in the
Netherlands for the English market during the first half of the
15th century. In its charming illustration of the Nativity, the
Virgin's bed in the stable is provided with curtains and
coverlet of mauve and green and her child is laid in a manger
that looks more like a gothic cradle. At her side Joseph stirs
broth in a pot on the fire. Only the ox and the ass suggest the
humble setting of the gospel story.

126 (opposite)

Travels of Sir John Mandeville

The author on the road to Constantinople

Bohemia, beginning of the 15th century.
No text; 225 x 180 mm, 16 fols.
Additional MS 24189, f.4b

One of the most popular books of the late Middle Ages was
the story of the exotic travel adventures of Sir John
Mandeville, which made its first appearance in the 1350s.
Mandeville was said to be an Englishman but the book draws
upon a wide range of earlier material and is particularly
focused on the Near East. It was translated into many
languages and widely copied. This miniature is one of a series
of 28 relating to the early chapters of the 'Travels', though
there is no accompanying text in the volume. They were
painted in Bohemia in the early years of the 15th century,
using an unusual technique of semi-grisaille on green-tinted
vellum, and provide a splendid impression of some of the
elaborate fashions in the clothing of the time.

127

Book of Hours

St George and the dragon

France, Paris, *c*.1407.
Latin; 225 x 160 mm, 319 fols.
Additional MS 29433, f.207

The principal illuminator of this manuscript is the Master of the Brussels Initials, trained in the Italian style of Niccolò da Bologna and his workshop (114, 117) but working here in a totally French idiom. General Italian influence is however apparent in the depiction of landscape and in the choice of naturalistic and grotesque themes among the marginal decoration. The artist takes his name from his appearance in the Duke of Berry's 'Très Belles Heures', now in the Bibliothèque Royale in Brussels.

128

Book of Hours

The Annunciation

France, Bourges, *c.*1405.
Latin; 190 x 140 mm, 198 fols.
Yates Thompson MS 37, f.19

Several of the leading French illuminators of the day
collaborated in the decoration of this book of hours. The text
is of the use of Bourges, principal place of residence of John,
Duke of Berry (died 1416), and most of the hands can also
be found in books made for his famous collection. The principal artist has been identified as the painter known as
Pseudo-Jacquemart. The influence of Italy is apparent in the
interest in perspective, the inclusion of naturalistic marginal
motifs and the choice of soft, yet bright, colours.

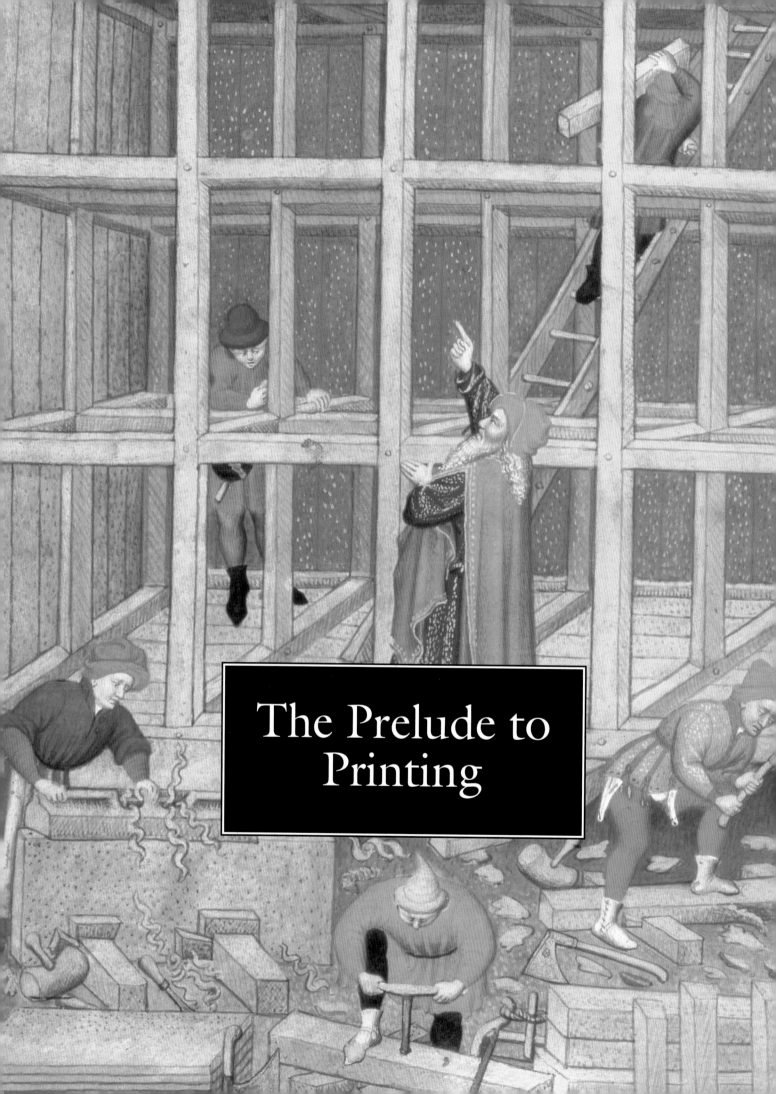

The Prelude to Printing

ery large numbers of illuminated manuscripts have come down to us from the 15th century, reflecting the tastes and requirements of a widely varied clientele, ranging from royalty to the lower ranks of the merchant classes. The degree to which books were decorated is equally varied, the most luxurious boasting dozens, occasionally hundreds, of individual images, the simplest a minimum of border decoration. The book of hours was the runaway best-seller, coveted as a fashionable symbol of personal devotion by all ranks of society. Other popular choices might include both devotional and secular texts for the bookshelf, with particular stress laid upon works with a historical flavour.

Book production during the early part of the century was dominated by the workshops of Paris, to which artists from other areas seem to have gravitated, adding their own local colour to current styles. The city produced work of quite extraordinary sophistication, its often dream-like quality enhanced by a rich, vivid but essentially unnatural palette of blue, green, rose and gold (129). The supporting marginal decoration is frequently as elaborate and colourful as the miniatures themselves (137). During the early years of the century the leading artists continued to enjoy the patronage of the French court. As most of them remain anonymous, they take their names from their principal customers (137), their best known works (129) or the books and writings with which they are particularly associated (136).

Anglo-French conflict continued during the reign of King Henry IV. In 1415 his son and successor, King Henry V, inflicted a crushing defeat upon a French army at Agincourt. In December 1415 the French king's eldest son died, followed not much more than a year later by his younger brother. In the autumn of 1419 the third and only surviving son was implicated in the assassination of his cousin, John the Fearless, Duke of Burgundy. He was repudiated by his parents and in 1420, under the terms of the Treaty of Troyes, the succession to the throne of France was ceded to the English king, who was to marry Charles VI's daughter, Catherine. An heir was born to the royal couple in December 1421. No one could have foretold that Henry V and Charles VI would both be dead before the child had reached his first birthday, leaving the government of both countries in the hands of a protracted regency.

During the third and fourth decades of the century Paris was thus subject to English rule and the illuminators' workshops which had supplied members of the French aristocracy found themselves working for English clients. Chief among the new patrons was John, Duke of Bedford, Henry V's younger brother, who was regent of France in the name of the infant Henry VI. Several magnificent illuminated books were made for him in Paris, in the workshop of a highly successful book painter who is known in his honour as

Detail from figure 148

the Bedford Master (138). Particularly handsome is the book of hours produced by this illuminator and his team to mark the marriage in 1423 of Bedford and Anne of Burgundy, daughter of John the Fearless, a political match designed to cement the alliance between England and the Burgundian Duke Philip the Good (148). The Bedford Master worked with several assistants who later followed independent careers and produced memorable work in their own right. When the English left Paris after Bedford's death in 1435, certain book painters chose to continue to work for them rather than for new clients. One at least, known as the Fastolf Master, seems to have left Paris to settle first in Normandy and ultimately in England itself (154). Others produced their later work for French patrons, including John, Count of Dunois, who had fought alongside Joan of Arc in 1429 (153).

In England itself the styles introduced at the beginning of the century, closely allied to work from the Low Countries and the lower Rhineland, remained current. The styles of some of the miniature painters working on books quite clearly written in England, such as those involved with the 'Big Bible' (133) or the Bedford Hours and Psalter (142), suggest that they may have been immigrants from these areas. The name of Hermann Scheerre, possibly a native of the lower Rhineland, has been associated with some of them. Substantial numbers of books of hours with liturgical features for use in England were imported from the continent, particularly from Flanders. French influence has been proposed for the grandest English hours of the period (140) and a German or Bohemian flavour can be distinguished in the charmingly illustrated English 'Life of St Edmund' produced for the young Henry VI soon after 1433 (151). Another work in English, the devotional treatise entitled 'The Desert of Religion', decorated in the north of England, includes facial types that look distinctly Dutch (149).

Dutch illuminators were enjoying a period of great prosperity, producing cycles of illustration for bibles and for books of hours translated into the vernacular and thus accessible to those unskilled in Latin (144, 156). These translations resulted from a great emphasis on the need for spiritual reading within the 'Devotio Moderna' introduced into the regular religious life by Geert Grote (died 1384) and widely adopted by lay members of the church. This movement was contemporary with that of Wycliffe and his Lollard disciples in England, and was soon followed by the activities of John Huss and his reformers in Bohemia. The Lollards and the Hussites were both viewed as politically dangerous and suffered severe persecution, while the 'Devotio Moderna' remained essentially a devotional movement. Nonetheless, all were in different ways manifestations of a more general dissatisfaction with both teaching and government in the established church of Rome, which was in schism from 1378 till 1417, with rival popes dividing the allegiance of Europe.

In Italy humanist scholars continued to seek out long-lost treasures of classical learning, following in the footsteps of Petrarch and Boccaccio. Their discoveries were translated, copied and circulated ever more widely to correspondents in other parts of Europe. One of the early followers of the movement in northern Europe was another of Henry V's brothers and an uncle of Henry VI, Humphrey, Duke of Gloucester (died 1447). Leonard Bruni's translation into Latin of Aristotle's *Politics* was originally dedicated to him, as was Pier Candido Decembrio's version of Plato's *Republic*. A firm supporter of the University of Oxford, he donated several hundred books to its library during the last decade of his life and the room in which manuscripts are read there still bears his name. At much the same time Henry VI himself was founding Eton College (1440) and King's College, Cambridge (1441), which assured him of two magnificent memorials.

The middle years of the 15th century were marked by a number of events representing either conclusions or new beginnings. In July 1453 the Hundred Years' War effectively came to an end when the army of King Charles VII finally overran the duchy of Aquitaine and the English commander, John Talbot, Earl of Shrewsbury was killed by the still innovatory power of cannon fire. In the same year Henry VI suffered an initial attack of insanity, the Duke of York was appointed regent and the power struggle between the houses of Lancaster and York, the Wars of the Roses, became inevitable. At the other end of Europe, Constantinople, ancient capital of the Byzantine Empire, finally fell to the Turks on 28 May 1453, after months of siege and a massive bombardment. Most significant however for the history of the book, the art of printing with moveable type, invented in Strasbourg in the late 1430s, was perfected at Mainz in the early 1450s by Johann Gutenberg. The completion of the enormous 42-line Bible in the summer of 1456 was a landmark achievement that was profoundly to affect the course of scholarship and culture within the next generation.

130 (above)

129 (opposite)

Guyart des Moulins: 'Bible Historiale'

God creating the world

France, Paris, c.1411.
French; 445 x 340 mm, 288 fols.
Royal MS 19 D. iii pt. 1, f.3

During the first quarter of the 15th century the workshops of Paris were famed throughout Europe for the richness, delicacy and variety of the work which they produced. This outstanding and very large miniature introduces the Book of Genesis in a two-volume copy of the 'Bible historiale' which was written out by Brother Thomas du Val, an Augustinian canon of the abbey of Clairefontaine in the diocese of Chartres. He recorded that he finished his task on 20 February 1411. Almost 150 illustrations were added professionally. This figure is in the style of an anonymous illuminator known as the Egerton Master on account of his contribution to a book of hours in the Egerton collection (134). He frequently collaborated with other fashionable book painters of the day, including the Boucicaut Master and his workshop (137).

Psalter of Henry VI

Christ and his disciples symbolically threatened with shipwreck

France, Paris, first decade of the 15th century with later additions.
Latin; 195 x 140 mm, 208 fols.
Cotton MS Domitian A. xvii, f.123

Two quite distinct series of miniatures punctuate this richly decorated psalter. One, showing groups of monks and nuns of various orders, was clearly added on extra leaves and in blank spaces, possibly about 1420. The other, of which this miniature is part, is integral to the original design of the book and dates from the early years of the century. Several of the early miniatures include the figure of a royal child, presented to Christ and the Virgin by various dignitaries, including St Louis of France and St Catherine. He is identified by his arms as the young Henry VI of England, who was born in December 1421. He cannot however have been the original owner and it has been suggested that the psalter was first owned by his mother's elder brother, the Dauphin Louis, who died in 1418.

131 (opposite)

Epistles and Treatises of St Jerome and Others

St Jerome and his companions; the Nativity, the Holy Trinity and the Resurrection

Italy, Bologna, *c*.1414.
Latin; 350 x 240 mm, 325 fols.
Egerton MS 3266, f.15

Although this volume was apparently written and largely decorated in Bologna, some of its illuminated pages are attributable to Michelino da Besozzo, one of the most celebrated Italian painters of his generation. Michelino, who did much of his work for the Visconti dukes of Milan, is known to have worked in many different media and was particularly famed for his wall paintings, most of which have unfortunately been destroyed. Several manuscripts illuminated by him have, however, been identified. This page, exemplifies the extraordinary grace of his figure style and his imaginative use of naturalistic plant forms.

132 (above)

Book of Hours

The patroness at prayer before the Virgin and Child

France, possibly Paris, *c*.1415.
Latin; 175 x 125 mm, 179 fols.
Harley MS 2952, ff. l9b–20

This book of hours probably commemorated the marriage of the lady portrayed in this miniature and an equally fashionable gentleman shown at prayer before the Virgin on the previous opening of the manuscript. Its artist, who worked within the circle of illuminators patronised by John, Duke of Berry, is particularly noted for his images of the Madonna of Humility and has thus attracted the title of Master of the Humilities. The remainder of the 41 miniatures in the manuscript are painted in grisaille with only touches of colour.

155

Bible

Initials introducing the Book of Malachi

England, probably London, early 15th century
(before March 1413).
Latin; 625 x 430 mm, 350 fols.
Royal MS 1 E. ix, f.239b (detail)

Conceived on a vast scale not unlike that of the great
bibles of the 12th century, this manuscript was made
by a group of artists working in England and generally, but probably erroneously, associated with the name
of Hermann Scheerre (122). The book has been traditionally linked with the name of King Richard II but
it has recently been suggested that it may be identifiable with the volume specifically described as a great
bible, 'magna biblia', which belonged to Henry IV.
That Bible was loaned by his son, Henry V, to the
Bridgettine nuns of the abbey of Syon, which he
founded early in 1415, shortly before he embarked
upon the Agincourt campaign.

134

Hours of René of Anjou

The Crucifixion

France, Paris, *c.*1410.
Latin; 220 x 160 mm, 154 fols.
Egerton MS 1070, f.116 (detail)

The Egerton Master (129) takes his name from his contribution to this manuscript, in which he was responsible for the principal miniatures. Much of the lesser decoration, including this small picture of the Crucifixion where tiny angels hover with chalices to catch Christ's blood, is in the style of the Boucicaut Master and his workshop. This talented book painter is now generally identified as Jacques Coene, a native of Bruges, who worked in Milan for the Visconti family at the very end of the 14th century and took with him to Paris the influence of Italian masters such as Michelino da Besozzo (131). The manuscript later belonged to René, Duke of Anjou, titular King of Jerusalem (died 1480), whose daughter Margaret married King Henry VI of England.

135

Burgundy Breviary (winter half)

Helsinus saved from drowning by the Virgin

North-eastern France, probably Paris, 1413–1419.
Latin and French; 245 x 180 mm, 438 fols.
Additional MS 35311, f.348b (detail)

John the Fearless, Duke of Burgundy, and his wife, Margaret of Bavaria, were the original owners of this two-volume breviary, the second part of which is now Harley MS 2897. The duke was a cousin of King Charles VI of France and, like him, a nephew of John, Duke of Berry. The illumination in the breviary is very much influenced by the work of John of Berry's most celebrated book painters, the Limbourg brothers, whose masterpiece is the world famous 'Très Riches Heures', now in the Musée Condé at Chantilly. They brought to French illumination a softness which distinguishes the work of their native Holland and contrasts with the more enamelled finish favoured by their Parisian contemporaries. John the Fearless died in 1419, assassinated on the bridge of Montereau by followers of the Dauphin.

136 (opposite)

Christine de Pisan: 'Collected Works'

Illustrations from the 'Epitre d'Othéa': Hercules and Jason, with their companions, threatened by Laomedon of Troy; Pyramus and Thisbe

France, Paris, c. 1410.
French; 370 x 285 mm, 398 fols.
Harley MS 4431, f. 112b

Christine de Pisan, one of the most widely famed French poets of the Middle Ages, was Italian by birth. Born in Venice in 1364, she was brought to France by her father at an early age when he was appointed astrologer to King Charles V. Her husband died in 1389, leaving her with three children to support, and she turned to her pen as a source of livelihood. She attracted important patrons, including Isabel of Bavaria, queen of Charles VI, for whom this elaborate copy of her works was made. The text was apparently written out by Christine herself. The illustrations were commissioned from an anonymous artist known as the Master of the 'Cité des Dames' in honour of his work on another of Christine's manuscripts.

137 (above)

Chevalier Hours

David penitent

France, Paris, c.1420.
Latin; 160 x 115 mm, 226 fols.
Additional MS 16997, f.90

All but one of the 17 large miniatures in this exceptionally beautiful manuscript are due to the Boucicaut Master, Jacques Coene, in his full maturity. Its rich colouring and delicate execution rank it among his finest works. The artist takes his pseudonym from the grand book of hours which was commissioned from him by Jean le Meingre de Boucicaut, Marshal of France, who was taken prisoner by the victorious English at Agincourt in 1415 and died in England in 1421. His manuscript is now in the Musée Jacquemart-André in Paris. The identity of the original owner of this book is not known, though the use of gold letters for the feast of St George in its calendar may suggest an English connection. The initials in the lower margin are those of Étienne Chevalier, patron of Jean Fouquet (163), who acquired it later in the 15th century.

159

138 (opposite)

Guyart des Moulins: 'Bible Historiale'

Frontispiece, incorporating scenes representing the Old and New Testaments

France, Paris, *c.*1420.
French; 460 x 330 mm, 296 fols.
Additional MS 18856, f.3

This elaborate composition, which includes figures of the four evangelists and representations of the Annunciation, the Assumption, the Ascension and Pentecost, is attributable to the Bedford Master. The artist takes his name from manuscripts which he illuminated for John, Duke of Bedford, the younger brother of King Henry V. He became Regent of France in the name of his infant nephew Henry VI in 1422. His Parisian workshop became extremely fashionable, working at times for both English and French clients (148, 152–154).

139 (above)

Petrus de Aureolis: 'Compendium super Bibliam'

The author preaching

England, possibly Lincoln with London additions, before 1422.
Latin; 350 x 235 mm, 131 fols.
Royal MS 8 G. iii, f.2 (detail)

According to a note at the front of this volume, dated February 1422, it was commissioned by Philip Repington, Bishop of Lincoln, for the new library of his cathedral, but reserved in the first instance for the use of Canon Richard Firsby. Firsby died in 1424 and the book duly reverted to the library, where it was entered in a 15th-century catalogue. The author, seen addressing his congregation in the introductory miniature, was a Franciscan who served as Archbishop of Aix in 1321–22. It is unusual for a manuscript of this kind to be given such elaborate decoration.

140 (opposite)

Hours of Elizabeth the Queen

Christ in the Garden of Gethsemane

England, London, *c*.1420–1430.
Latin; 205 x 150 mm, 154 fols.
Additional MS 50001, f.10b

Brilliantly illustrated with 18 half-page miniatures and several
hundred initials, large and small, ornamented with lifelike
human heads, this manuscript has been described as the finest
English book of its period. The principal artist, responsible
for almost all the miniatures, was strongly influenced by
continental work, both French and Flemish. The second hand
is also to be found in the Bedford Hours and Psalter (142).
The identity of the original patron is not known but an added
prayer for the soul of Cecily Neville, Duchess of Warwick
(died 1450) suggests a link with her family. Elizabeth of
York, Henry VII's queen, wrote her name in the book later in
the century, which gives it the name by which it is popularly

141 (above)

Alain Chartier: 'Le Livre des Quatre Dames'

The author with the four ladies

France, *c*.1425.
French; 245 x 165 mm, 71 fols.
Additional MS 21247, f.1

Alain Chartier, born in Bayeux about 1395, was secretary to
the French King Charles VI and his son, afterwards Charles
VII. His earliest verse was composed about 1414 and this
particular work dates from shortly after the Battle of
Agincourt in 1415. The four ladies of the title relate the fates
of four gentlemen caught up in the battle, one dead, one lost,
one taken prisoner and the fourth saved by flight. The arms
in the initial are those of the Montmorency family, staunch
supporters of the French crown.

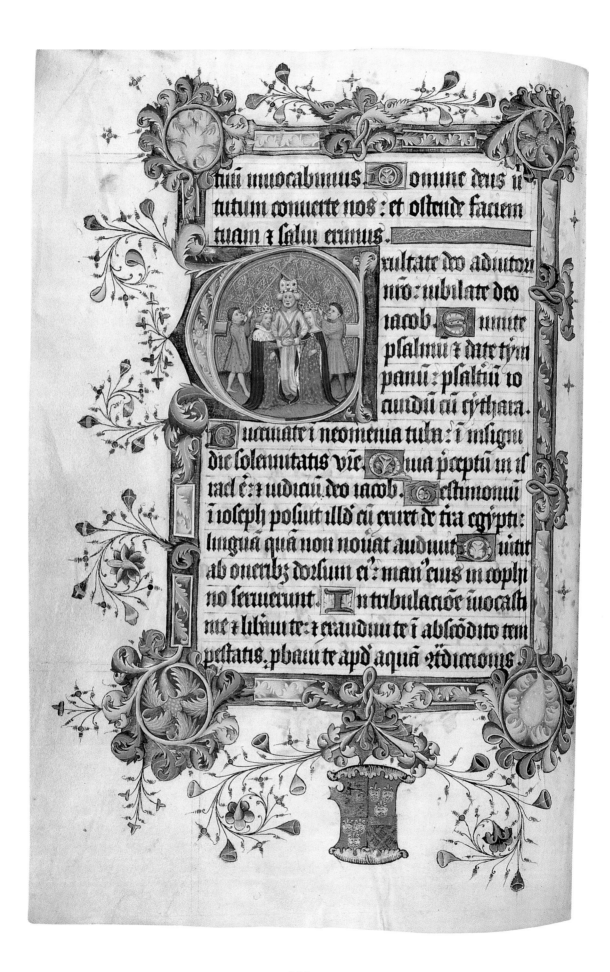

142 (opposite)

Bedford Hours and Psalter

The marriage of King David

England, London, after 1414 and probably before 1423.
Latin; 405 x 280 mm, 240 fols.
Additional MS 42131, f.151b

Totally unknown to scholars before 1928, this very grand book was made for John, Duke of Bedford, younger brother of King Henry V, after he had been granted the Bedford title and probably before his marriage to Anne of Burgundy in 1423. It contains some of the finest English illumination of its time, part of which may be attributable to Hermann Scheerre (122). The unusual illustration of the marriage of David, shown in contemporary royal dress, may be a reference to the marriage of Henry V and Princess Catherine of France, which took place in 1420. The arms at the foot of the page were added later in the 15th century when the book belonged to William Catesby, a close associate of Richard III.

143 (above)

Missal for Special Feastdays

Crucifixion marking the canon of the Mass; the patron at the feet of the Virgin and Child

Germany, Cologne, early 15th century.
Latin; 260 x 185 mm, 130 fols.
Egerton MS 3018, ff. 23b–24

The destination of this unusual manuscript was apparently the church of St Severinus in Cologne. A Mass for his feastday is included and other Cologne saints appear in the calendar. The arms of the patron are no longer legible. Most of the text is written in an Italianate hand, though the specifically Cologne material is by a Rhenish scribe. The seven full-page miniatures, added on separate leaves, were certainly painted in Germany. The canon page is probably also German, though heavily influenced by Italian work. The whole manuscript exemplifies the often confusing combinations of style found in north European manuscripts of this date.

144

145

Book of Hours

Soldiers casting lots over Christ's garments

Holland, possibly Delft, *c*.1420.
Dutch; 125 x 90 mm, 179 fols.
Additional MS 50005, f.119b

This remarkable little book of hours contains no less than
66 miniatures of scenes from the life of Christ and the Virgin
Mary, carried out in an ink and wash technique that is
sometimes heightened with patches of gold. Large in
proportion to the pages of the manuscript, the figures are
shown in contemporary dress and have a liveliness and
immediacy uncommon in more elaborately painted books.
The principal artist, who apparently specialised in the
production of books of hours, is known as the Master of the
Morgan Infancy Cycle, from an example of his work in the
Pierpont Morgan Library, New York. His style suggests a
connection with the printed block books of the period.

Book of Hours

Susannah and the elders

Germany, Lower Rhineland, *c*.1420–1425.
German; 240 x 170 mm, 41 detached folios.
Egerton MS 859, f.31

Influenced by the work of the leading illuminators of Paris as
well as by those of the neighbouring Netherlands, the artists
of this once elaborate but now unfortunately dismembered
book produced a series of charmingly naïve and often dramatic illustrations of saints and biblical episodes to accompany a
vernacular devotional text. It has been suggested that the
original owner, who appears on another page of the
manuscript bearing a rather damaged coat of arms, may have
been Mary, Duchess of Cleves, one of the daughters of John
the Fearless, Duke of Burgundy, and his wife Margaret of
Bavaria (135).

146 (previous page)

Bible

Opening page of the Book of Genesis: the days of creation; marginal figures of the priest-king Melchisedek, of Augustine and Aristotle and of Albertus Magnus and Averroes

Flanders, Liège, *c*.1430.
Latin; 515 X 370 mm, 289 fols.
Additional MS 15254, f.13

Only two pages of this five-volume bible are illuminated. Here the first page of the main text is provided with what amounts to a pictorial commentary, featuring figures of famous scholars and theologians with extracts from their writings. The illumination is very striking and cannot be directly related to any other work. The manuscript was at the Benedictine monastery of St Jacques in Liège in the mid 17th century and it is likely that it was in fact produced locally.

148 (opposite)

Bedford Hours

The building of Noah's Ark

France, Paris, *c*.1423.
Latin and French; 260 x 180 mm, 289 fols.
Additional MS 18850, f.15b

This magnificent book of hours, which gives its name to one of the leading Parisian book painters of the period (138), was written and illuminated for John, Duke of Bedford and his wife Anne, younger sister of Philip, Duke of Burgundy, probably on the occasion of their marriage in 1423. Arranged to cement an alliance between England and Burgundy, the match blossomed into one of the greatest love affairs of the time. The manuscript contains more than 1200 marginal scenes from the Bible in addition to the large miniatures which traditionally punctuate its text. This picture, which is the work of one of the Bedford Master's chief collaborators, the Master of the Munich Golden Legend (152), forms part of a special Old Testament sequence at the beginning of the volume.

147

Ulrich von Pottenstein: 'Spiegel der Weisheit'

The fable of the goat and the hedgehog

Austria, *c*.1415–1425.
German; 260 x 190 mm, 127 fols.
Egerton MS 1121, f.44b (detail)

Ulrich von Pottenstein was chaplain to the Austrian Duke Albrecht IV. He made this German translation of a collection of Latin fables about 1415. The original is thought to have been produced during the 13th century and includes fables reminiscent of Aesop, with stories related to the bestiary and to the adventures of Reynard the Fox. The narrative is very ponderous, with long dialogues full of learned remarks quite unsuited to the characters of the animals to which they are attributed. The illustrations in this copy are, however, both animated and lifelike.

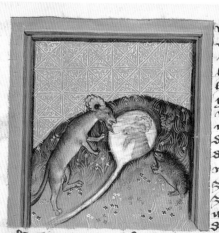

Coinment leig comenda a noel fair vne arrle er y mettre vne paire de tout lrstes pur le deluge

149 (above)

The Desert of Religion

The futility of worldly achievement in the face of death

Northern England, second quarter of the 15th century.
English; 255 x 200 mm, 23 fols.
Cotton MS Faustina B. vi, ff.1b–2

The presence of two Yorkshire saints, Richard Rolle of
Hampole (died 1349) and the 7th-century abbess Hilda of
Whitby, among the figures illustrating the main text of this
volume, associate it very clearly with the north-east of
England. Stylistically it betrays a relationship with contemporary glass painting and the facial types suggest a link with
Germany and the Netherlands. This double-page frontispiece
underlines the futility of worldly rank and achievement in the
face of death. On the left are representatives of the highest
ranks of society. On the right Christ and his mother petition
God the Father to pardon the sins of a dying man. He is
threatened by a waiting devil who proclaims: 'This saule i
chalange for to wyne, which i knawe is ful of syne.'

150 (opposite)

Prophecies of the Popes

A fortified city, representing Rome

Italy, Florence, c.1431–1447.
Latin; 285 x 195 mm, 15 fols.
Harley MS 1340, f.12

Immensely popular during the late Middle Ages and
Renaissance, this text is commonly attributed to Joachim,
abbot of Fiore (died 1202) and Anselm, bishop of Marsico
(died about 1210). It was, however, almost certainly composed about a century later than their time. A great many
illustrated copies are known. This one was probably produced
between 1431 and 1447, as the last named pope is Eugenius
IV. Its artist was very much influenced by Fra Angelico (died
1455), most of whose work was done in Florence. His style is
close to that of Benozzo Gozzoli (1420–97) and it has been
suggested that these miniatures are the youthful work of one
of Gozzoli's contemporaries, the artist of the San Miniato
altarpiece.

Et miser suſtineas paſſiones cuictas miſerabile ut appareat lumen morti tenebit
cura parnum tepus cetens enī inte effuſio ſaguinū romary incipietes nō reficient
ſi quinq̃ principatus a monarchia tua draconem confringet que occīet labin fruſtatus
laniabunt membra illi no ceſa rad pugnā inteſtina incitata rmirabile multitudi
nem cetens gladio ad miliaria ſex ſeptem numerata romis implicitas fornicator ce
tres maculatus rdaulter raptor in iuſtus ſorgdomita urcebut ultimū luī ante oculos :~

ſſoteſtas cenobia ad locum paſtorum redibunt : :~

151

John Lydgate: 'Life of St Edmund'

King Sweyn on his deathbed; a sinful woman prevented from approaching St Edmund's shrine

England, Bury St Edmunds or London, after 1433.
English; 250 x 170 mm, 119 fols.
Harley MS 2278, ff.105b–106

John Lydgate, who died about 1450, was a monk of Bury St Edmunds and court poet to King Henry V and his son, Henry VI. This copy of his verse life of St Edmund was written and illuminated by order of the abbot as a gift for 12-year-old Henry VI after he had spent Christmas at Bury in 1433. No exact parallel has been found for the idiosyncratic style of its illuminator. He seems to have been familiar not only with contemporary English work but also with material from Holland, France, Germany and Bohemia. He has a lively sense of narrative and seems to have enjoyed depicting rich fabrics and tiny details.

152

Book of Hours

The Last Judgement

France, Paris, *c.*1436.
Latin and French; 195 x 130 mm, 244 fols.
Additional MS 181921, f.89b

Known as the Master of the Golden Legend in honour of one of his
most ambitious works, now in Munich, this artist was at one time a
member of the same team as the Bedford Master. He worked
variously for both English and French patrons and was responsible
for a series of panel portraits of members of the Neville family. The
fashionably dressed original owner is portrayed in the margin alongside the miniature. She is seen several times in the book, occasionally
accompanied by her husband and sons. Her emblem was an ermine
and her motto 'Souvenir'. Unfortunately all trace of her coat of arms
has been obliterated. Its shadowy shape may be seen here beneath
the clump of daisies in the lower margin.

153

Hours of Jean Dunois

The discovery and exaltation of the Cross

France, Paris, after 1436.
Latin and French; 135 x 95 mm, 291 fols.
Yates Thompson MS 3, f.184

This extraordinarily rich and very elegant little book of hours was made for Jean, Count of Dunois, known as the Bastard of Orléans (died 1468), probably soon after the French regained control of Paris in 1436. Its principal artist was a close associate of the Bedford Master (138), whose distinctive style he echoes, and has been named the Dunois Master in honour of this manuscript. The book contains 60 large miniatures, many of which are supplemented by related marginal scenes such as this one of St Helena discovering the True Cross. Every one of its pages has its margins elaborately painted with flowers and foliage. It seems almost unsuitably delicate for a man who was a professional soldier and the companion in arms of Joan of Arc.

174

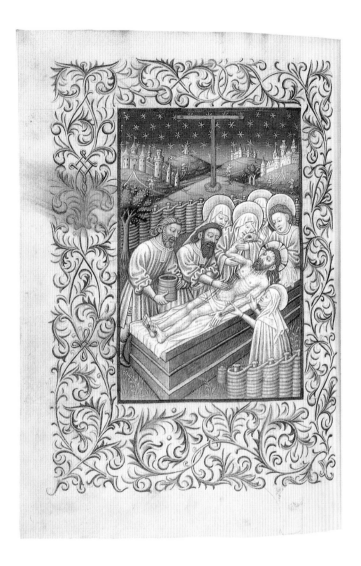

154

Book of Hours

Christ laid in the tomb

England, by a French artist, *c.*1450.
Latin and French; 175 x 125 mm, 191 fols.
Harley MS 2915, f.173b

The illuminator of this book was yet another of the artists
whose early work appears in manuscripts from the workshop
of the Bedford Master. He is known as the Fastolf Master
because his chief patron was Sir John Fastolf, an English
soldier and public servant in France during the early part of
the reign of Henry VI. He apparently left Paris to work for
the English occupiers of Normandy before crossing the
Channel to England, where he became associated with a fine
calligrapher named Ricardus Franciscus with whom he
worked on several books, including this one. Most of his
work is very brightly coloured but here he demonstrates great
subtlety in the use of a semi-grisaille technique.

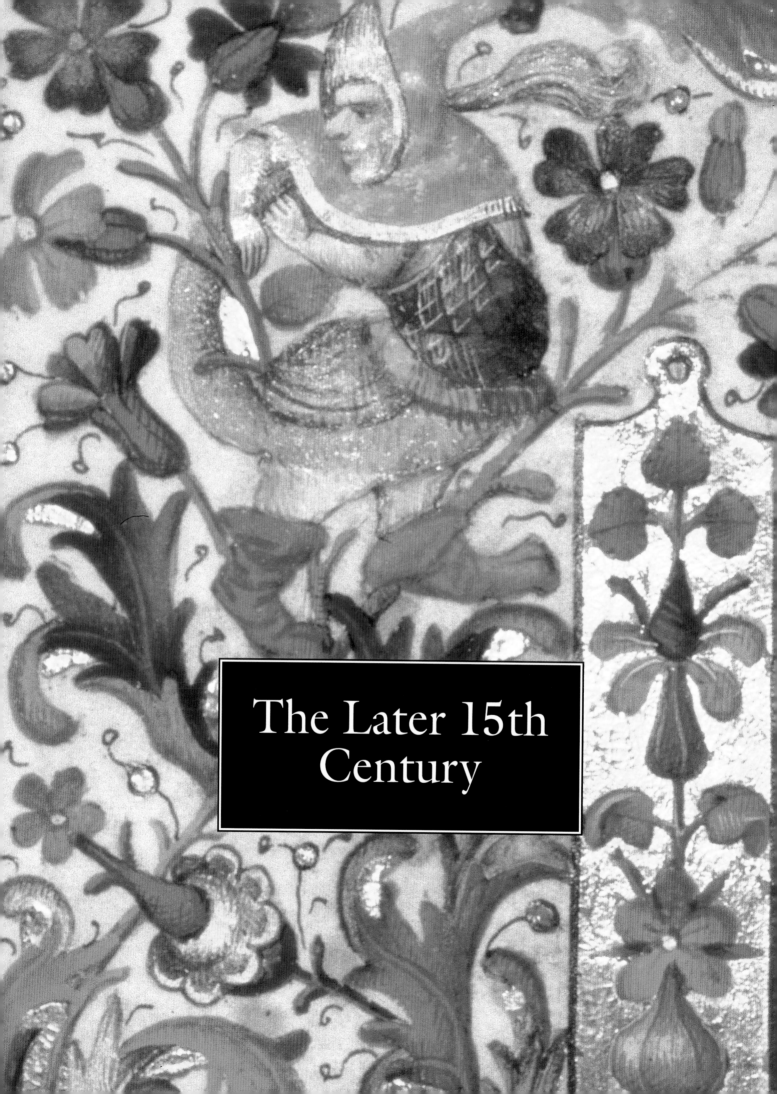

The Later 15th Century

From the standpoint of the late 20th century the profound signif-icance of the publication of Gutenberg's 42-line bible is clearly apparent. In its own day the new process for the multiplication of texts, involving the first ever use of moveable type on an ambi-tious scale, certainly aroused widespread interest. Its potential for obviating the repetitive work of traditional methods of book production was quickly recognised. Copies of the printed bible made their way to many places outside Germany and some were enhanced by the addition of illumi-nated decoration in appropriate local styles. The technique which had pro-duced the book was rapidly adopted in other centres and printing presses were established in Italy in 1465, in France in 1470 and in England in 1476. England's first printer, William Caxton, learned his skills in Cologne and produced his first books in Bruges under the patronage of the English Duchess of Burgundy, Margaret of York (died 1503). He was to achieve a special place in the history of English vernacular literature for his publica-tions in English, notably his editions of *The Canterbury Tales* (in 1478 and 1483, the second edition illustrated with woodcuts of the pilgrims) and of the *Morte d'Arthur* (1485). It was however to be some considerable time before the impact of the new process began to be felt by the book trade in general, and the widespread demand for fine manuscripts so apparent during the first half of the 15th century continued undiminished. The lavish work produced in Germany itself at about this time is represented by a missal made for a bishop of Würzburg (155), at no great distance from Gutenberg's own workshop in Mainz.

In northern Italy (159, 161), in southern Italy (158) and in Spain (164, 166, 167) elaborately and traditionally ornamented books of private devo-tion continued to offer illuminators their most frequent opportunities for lavish decoration and expensive cycles of illustration. In Savoy, lying between Italy and France, the patronage of the ducal court encouraged several distin-guished book painters to settle (162). In France itself, although Paris con-tinued to play a leading role in the production of illuminated books (172) and many of the regions developed distinctive schools of illumination of their own, the focal point shifted to the valley of the river Loire. There, King Charles VII, crowned at Reims in 1429 under the protection of Joan of Arc but for many years denied access to the traditional capital by the continued presence of the English, had set up court at Bourges.

The artists patronised by Charles VII and his court included Jean Fouquet, a great original genius, whose influence dominated French paint-ing during the second half of the 15th century and beyond. Because he can be identified by name and not merely as a stylistic personality, and because substantial numbers of relevant documents have survived, it is possible to fol-low his career in some detail and to see the influences at work on his devel-

Detail from figure 162

opment. Fouquet seems to have been born at Tours about 1420. He is known to have visited Rome during the 1440s and while there painted a portrait of Pope Eugenius IV. His experiences during this journey, when he must have met a number of contemporary artists and seen examples of work being produced in Italy, are certainly reflected in his own later work. Portrait painting was one of his strengths and he was responsible for the best-known image of Charles VII (now in the Louvre in Paris). Like the majority of court-based artists, he also undertook designs and large-scale works in connection with public festivities; he designed the tomb of Charles's successor, Louis XI. His finest works are, however, to be found in illuminated manuscripts and include ambitious historical illustrations as well as devotional subjects. His masterpiece is the magnificent book of hours, now tragically dismembered and incomplete, commissioned by Etienne Chevalier, a leading royal administrator who became Treasurer of France in 1452 (163). As befitted an artist of his standing, Fouquet had a number of pupils and assistants working alongside him. He died at some time before 8 November 1481, when mention is made of his widow, but his influence persisted into the 16th century, passed down through the work of such successors as Jean Bourdichon (187). The Loire valley also produced the extremely successful and stylistically distinctive Jean Colombe (179), whose prolific output included substantial commissions from the ducal family of Savoy.

The second half of the century is also noted for a great blossoming of the trade in illuminated books through the Netherlands. Dutch and Flemish illuminators working at the beginning of the century had supplied customers elsewhere (124, 125) and craftsmen trained in the Low Countries had migrated to workshops in England and in France. A major school of panel painting emerged in the Low Countries, beginning with the work of Jan Van Eyck. He is known to have been employed by John of Bavaria, Count of Holland, in the early 1420s, and to have moved into the circle of Philip the Good, Duke of Burgundy in 1425. In 1430 he settled finally at Bruges, where he enjoyed the patronage of some of the resident Italian merchants. The completion of his masterpiece, the Ghent altarpiece of the Adoration of the Lamb, in which he is associated with his brother Hubert, is dated 1432 and he died at Bruges in 1441. He was followed by a succession of major painters, including Petrus Christus, Rogier van der Weyden, Dieric Bouts, Hugo van der Goes and Hans Memling. All of these artists, alongside their contemporaries among the book painters, benefited from a combination of the patronage of the Flemish court of the Burgundian dukes and that of the international community of merchants based in Bruges and other Flemish cities, which constituted a clearing house for European trade.

Duke Philip the Good, founder in 1430 of the Order of the Golden Fleece (178) and a noted bibliophile who patronised all the leading illuminators of the region in his campaign to build up a library worthy of the ducal house of Burgundy, died in the summer of 1467. His son, Duke Charles the Bold, almost at once set about cementing an alliance with the English Yorkist

King Edward IV, who had ousted the Lancastrian Henry VI in 1461. Such an alliance was of considerable commercial as well as political significance, since the Burgundian Netherlands provided a vital link in the English wool trade. Charles took as his third wife the English king's sister, Margaret of York (170), who lived out the remainder of her life in the Low Countries and played a notable political role, especially after the early death of her husband at the beginning of 1477 (171). Edward was offered sanctuary in Flanders in 1470–71 during the temporary return to power of Henry VI and his supporters. And his experiences then as the guest of Louis de Gruthuyse (173), coupled with his knowledge of the ducal library through the medium of his sister, probably coloured his own patronage of some of the workshops of Bruges when he set about ordering grand illuminated books for his own use in the late 1470s (frontispiece, 177, 180). These very large and very colourful manuscripts represent the first ever documented campaign of selective acquisition for the English royal library.

Edward IV's library books have often been compared unfavourably with similar volumes emanating from other major libraries of the time, notably those collected by the Burgundian dukes. Many of the major illuminators active somewhat earlier in the century, such as Vrelant (165), were no longer available when he entered the market. The most talented of the book painters active during the late 1470s and the 1480s did not necessarily undertake the miniatures required as illustrations for secular books but instead concentrated their talents on liturgical works and in particular on books of hours (175, 181). During the last years of the 15th century the workshops of Bruges and nearby Ghent became famous throughout Europe for a flood of exquisite devotional manuscripts, their texts punctuated by scenes from the gospels and the lives of the saints, their borders filled with illusionistic flowers and insects or with vignettes of contemporary courtly life. These manuscripts were commissioned by customers from many countries, thanks to the international composition of the merchant communities, and were dispatched along with panels by Hugo van der Goes or Hans Memling for use in households in various centres both north and south, where their presence added a Flemish ingredient to the experience of local painters and illuminators.

155 (opposite)

Missal

The Crucifixion

Germany, Würzburg, mid 15th century.
Latin; 440 x 330 mm, 303 fols.
Arundel MS 108, f.146b

The figures of the crucified Christ, his mother and his favourite disciple, St John, are placed against a background of heavy tooled gold, protected by a curtain of purple silk stitched to the vellum page. Their robes are painted in the soft, bright colours favoured by German illuminators of the time and the ground at their feet is studded with delicately painted naturalistic plants. The manuscript was made for use at Würzburg in the time of Gottfried von Limpurg, who was bishop between 1443 and 1455.

156 (above)

History Bible

The crossing of the Red Sea

Northern Netherlands, c.1440.
Dutch; 390 x 290 mm, 300 fols.
Additional MS 15410, f.54 (detail)

Dutch miniature painters produced a substantial number of illustrated copies of a vernacular version of the bible, the most elaborate containing more than 500 separate miniatures. This bible, made about 1440, was painted by the Master of Catherine of Cleves and his associates. Much admired and studied since the rediscovery of his masterpiece, the Hours of Catherine of Cleves, Duchess of Guelders, in the early 1960s, this artist's style has been identified in a large number of manuscripts. The Hours is now one of the greatest treasures of the Pierpont Morgan Library in New York. This miniature, though not by the Master's own hand, is a fine and lively example of the work being produced in the northern Netherlands during his time.

157 (opposite)

'Le Livre de la Fleur des Histoires de la Terre d'Orient'

The Tartars seen installing and honouring their leader

North-eastern France, *c*.1440–1450.
French; 285 x 210 mm, 86 fols.
Additional MS 17971, f.23

The arms in the initial with which the text opens are those of Jean V de Créquy, a native of Artois, counsellor and chamberlain to Duke Philip the Good of Burgundy and one of the first members of the Order of the Golden Fleece, to which he was admitted in 1430. He was also a bibliophile for whom the artist of this manuscript painted several volumes around the middle of the 15th century. The rather unusual text is said to have been compiled at Poitiers in 1307 by a cousin of the king of Armenia, at the command of Pope Clement V.

158 (above)

Prayerbook of Alfonso V of Aragon

Aragon or possibly Naples, *c*.1442.
Latin; 225 x 165 mm, 427 fols.
Additional MS 28962, f.78

Rich in pictorial references to himself and to his family, Alfonso's prayerbook probably celebrates his acquisition of the kingdom of Naples in 1442. He was well known as a scholar and as a connoisseur of fine books and founded one of the greatest libraries of the Renaissance, further developed by his son and successor, Ferdinand I of Naples, who reigned from 1458 till 1494. This miniature refers to the ongoing struggle against the Moors, who still occupied much of southern Spain and who were finally overcome only with the conquest of Granada in 1492. A figure representing Alfonso himself, clad in the scarlet and gold armorial colours of Aragon, leads the Christian forces into battle.

159

Psalter

Figure of an angel

Italy, Pavia, *c.*1450.
Latin; 135 x 100 mm, 276 fols.
Additional MS 15114, f.48b

Belbello da Pavia, the leading Lombard illuminator of the day, was responsible for the miniatures in this richly decorated small psalter. Patronised by a wealthy clientele that included such grandees as the dukes of Milan and the marquises of Ferrara and Mantua, he produced intense and dramatic miniatures, heavily lit with gold. His figure style looks back to the French masters of the early years of the century but his frequent use of solid gold backgrounds as a foil for his figures suggests the influence of Byzantine art.

160

Plutarch: 'Parallel Lives'

Emilius Paulus and Nasica discover fresh water at the foot of Mount Olympus

Italy, Milan, *c.*1450–1460.
Latin; 335 x 240 mm, 240 fols.
Additional MS 22318, f.106 (detail)

The text of Plutarch's 'Parallel Lives' was translated from the Greek by Leonardo Bruni and others during the first quarter of the 15th century. This is a particularly lavish copy, which suggests that it was intended for an important patron. The illumination, which was never completed, is the work of three different north Italian artists who have not been identified. Stylistically this miniature, with its fantastic landscape heavily enhanced with gold, is close to the work of Belbello da Pavia (159).

161

Book of Hours

St Anne teaching her daughter, the Virgin Mary,
to read

Northern Italy, third quarter of the 15th century.
Latin; 125 x 90 mm, 360 fols.
Additional MS 22569, f.65b

Small in scale but written in a very large script, this manuscript was clearly intended for the private devotional use of an
individual. Its calendar includes the feast days of St Zeno,
Bishop of Verona, but it also has a partially erased colophon
naming a Franciscan friar called Gregorio Pasqui of Florence.
Its exact origin thus remains in doubt. Several of its miniatures illustrate apocryphal incidents from the life of the
Virgin. The subject of St Anne teaching her daughter to read
was universally popular during the later Middle Ages.

163 (above)

Hours of Etienne Chevalier

David penitent

France, Tours, *c.*1452–1460.
Latin; 195 x 150 mm, single detached leaf.
Additional MS 37421

162 (opposite)

Saluces Hours

The martyrdom of St Catherine

Savoy, mid 15th century.
Latin; 280 x 195 mm, 219 fols.
Additional MS 27697, f.200b

Large in format for a book of hours, this manuscript is one of a number of outstanding illuminated books produced by artists working for the court of Savoy during the middle of the 15th century. Every one of its pages is surrounded by an elaborate border and it contains 34 large miniatures, many of unusual subjects. Several different hands contributed to the book. The most important of them, responsible for this miniature, has recently been identified as Antoine de Lonhy, who arrived in the area only in 1462, having previously been documented working in Barcelona. The book takes its name from an apparent association with the family of Mainfroy de Saluces, Marshal of Savoy (died 1455), whose arms appear in the volume.

Jean Fouquet, born in Tours about 1420, was the greatest French painter of the 15th century. This miniature comes from his masterpiece, the Hours of Etienne Chevalier, now represented only by a series of 47 detached miniatures, 40 of which are among the treasures of the Musée Condé at Chantilly. Chevalier was a secretary to King Charles VII of France, whose court was based at Tours, and became treasurer of France in 1452. He died in 1474. Fouquet, who is known to have visited Italy as a young man, was renowned for the lifelike quality of his art and the sureness with which he handled space and distance. Surviving work from his hand includes secular as well as devotional books and also paintings on panel.

164

Book of Hours

The Resurrection

Spain, mid 15th century.
Latin; 195 x 140 mm, 168 fols.
Egerton MS 2653, f.75

The script and decoration of this manuscript seem at first sight to be noticeably later in date than its miniatures, all of which are painted on sheets of vellum individually inserted into the volume at unusual intervals. Spanish book painting was, however, very heavily indebted to outside models. Influences from France, Italy, the Low Countries and even Bohemia may be recognised in Spanish books, leading to confusion in dates and styles. Some of the miniatures in this manuscript have similarities with the Prayerbook of Alfonso V of Aragon (158), which is dated about 1442.

165

Bregilles Hours

The Crucifixion

Flanders, Bruges, *c*.1460.
Latin; 190 x 130 mm, 210 fols.
Yates Thompson MS 4, f.27

Delicately illuminated throughout in grisaille, this book of hours contains five miniatures and 26 historiated initials in the fashionable Bruges style of the middle of the 15th century. One of the miniatures, this beautiful crucifixion, is attributable to Guillaume Vrelant, who dominated the production of illuminated manuscripts in Bruges during the third quarter of the 15th century. Born in Utrecht, he had migrated south by 1454 and was the founder of the Bruges Guild of Illuminators. The original owner of the book was Jacob de Bregilles, who died in Brussels in 1475.

166

Book of Hours

Pièta

Spain, Toledo, late 15th century.
Latin; 205 x 175 mm, 87 fols.
Additional MS 50004, f.70b

The unknown owner of this book of hours was a lady named 'Amise'. The manuscript is far from complete and a further fragment is now in the Kupferstichkabinett in Berlin. Lavishly decorated in a style that owes much to the influence of Flemish book painting and especially to the work of Guillaume Vrelant (165), it represents the highly stylised product of Spanish illuminators around 1480. This particular workshop was apparently in Toledo.

167

Book of Hours

Celebration of the Office of the Dead

Spain, second half of the 15th century (after 1461).
Latin; 195 x 135 mm, 153 fols.
Additional MS 18193, ff.86b–87

The Spanish lady who originally owned this book is depicted
within its pages, kneeling at the feet of St Mary Magdalene
who was presumably her patron. The inclusion of the feast of
St Catherine of Siena places its execution after her
canonisation in 1461. The style of the border decoration is
clearly influenced by Flemish work of the middle of the
century but some of the miniatures reflect a knowledge of
Italian manuscripts. In this unusual miniature the fates of the
blessed and the damned are shown as the subjects of the
paintings behind the altar.

168

Genesis in Pictures

*Joseph interpreting the dreams of Pharaoh's butler
and baker*

Southern Netherlands, second half of the 15th century.
French; 265 x 190 mm, 132 fols.
Additional MS 39657, f.108b

Bible picture books, sometimes in manuscript but with
increasing frequency produced by one of the up-to-date
printing techniques, were popular during the 15th century
and were probably often used as teaching aids. The text
accompanying the pictures in this volume is drawn from a
French Bible History current about the middle of the
century. The coloured line drawings, executed on paper, are
very reminiscent of the work of Dutch and German wood
engravers of the period.

169

'Historie van Jason; Dat Scaecspel'

Holland, possibly Haarlem, *c.*1475–1480.
Dutch; 270 x 200 mm, 226 fols.
Additional MS 10290, f.171b

Two quite separate works are bound together in this volume,
written and painted on paper at the beginning of the third
quarter of the 15th century. The first part, the Dutch
translation of Raoul Lefèvre's French 'History of Jason', was
used as a model by the Haarlem printer Jacob Bellaert about
1485. This figure of an enthroned queen is one of the
illustrations to the second part, a Dutch adaptation of the
'Ludus Scaccorum' of Jacob de Cessolis. Both works enjoyed
a wide circulation and were variously translated. Both were
printed for an English audience by William Caxton, *The
History of Jason* in 1477 with a dedication to the young
Prince of Wales, and *The Game and Play of Chess*, illustrated
with woodcuts, in 1482.

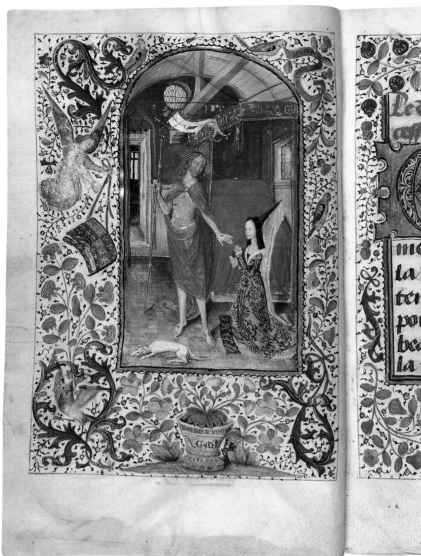

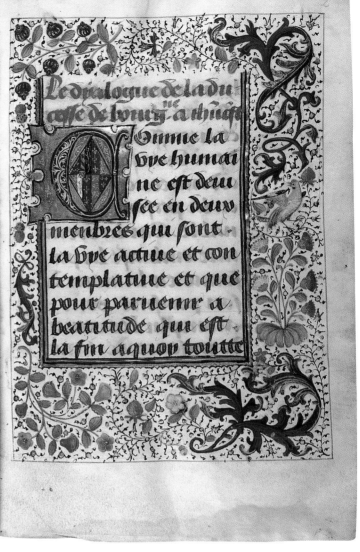

170 (above)

'Le Dialogue de Jesus christ et la Duchesse'

Margaret of York, kneeling at the feet of Christ

Flanders, Ghent or Bruges, *c.*1470.
French; 200 x 140 mm, 142 fols.
Additional MS 7970, ff.1b–2

Princess Margaret of York, sister of King Edward IV of England, married Charles, Duke of Burgundy, as his third wife in 1468, cementing an alliance between the two powers. The marriage celebrations were of unprecedented magnificence and set a standard for all Europe for the remainder of the century. The new duchess was a learned and devout lady, and she commissioned a number of splendid illuminated manuscripts from the craftsmen of Ghent and Bruges. Her arms, impaling those of her husband, and her personal emblem of the daisy (marguerite), are included in the decoration of these pages.

171 (opposite)

Ordinance of Charles the Bold

The Duke receiving the oath of allegiance from his military captains

Flanders, possibly Brussels, *c.*1474–1476.
French; 305 x 216 mm, 41 fols.
Additional MS 36619, f.5

This manuscript contains the ordinance of Charles the Bold, Duke of Burgundy, for the regulation of his military levies, dated at Trier in the autumn of 1473. The miniature is surrounded by an elaborate border which incorporates the arms of his six duchies, nine counties, one marquisate and three other lordships. His own arms are at the foot of the page, surrounded by the collar of the Order of the Golden Fleece, and a monogram joining his initial with that of his wife, Margaret, appears several times. Charles died in battle shortly after this manuscript was written, defeated by the Swiss at Nancy on 5 January 1477.

174

Missal

The Annunciation

Italy, Padua or Tuscany, after 1479.
Latin; 410 x 280 mm, 294 fols.
Additional MS 30038, f.209 (detail)

Decorated with more than 70 historiated initials enclosing scenes from the bible and figures of individual saints, together with numerous purely ornamental initials composed of brightly coloured foliage, this manuscript was long attributed on stylistic grounds to Spain. In fact it was made for the priory of St Mary and St Helen at Padua, after that house had been transferred to the Olivetan order by Pope Sixtus IV in 1479. The figure of a donor appears on the rather damaged opening page and the accompanying coats of arms suggest that he was a member of the Borromeo family of Florence and Padua.

172 (previous pages, left)

Valerius Maximus: 'Memorabilia'

Scenes from Roman history

France, Paris, c.1475.
French; 475 x 350 mm, 253 fols.
Harley MS 4374, f.161

Designed on an extremely lavish scale and copiously illustrated, this copy of the 'Memorabilia' of Valerius Maximus belonged to the French historian Philippe de Comines (died 1511). His arms appear in the top left-hand corner of the composition and his initial, joined with that of his wife, Hélène de Chambres-Montsoreau, whom he married in 1473, is on the architectural frame. The text of the volume is a French translation of the Latin original, made at the end of the 14th century by Simon de Hesdin and Nicholas de Gonesse. The miniature, in a style associated with the names of Maître François and Jacques de Besançon, a late descendant of the Bedford Master workshop, shows the bravery of the young Emilius Lepidus in battle, the horror of the child Marcus Cato at the cruelties of Sulla, and Julius Caesar gazing at the decapitated bodies of Pompey's nephews and of Faustus Sulla and his wife Pompeia.

173 (previous pages, right)

Jean de Wavrin: 'Chroniques d'Angleterre'

The camp of Brutus on the river Loire

Flanders, Bruges, 1470s.
French; 450 x 350 mm, 350 fols.
Royal MS 15 E. iv, f.36

Wavrin dedicated his chronicle to King Edward IV of England and this magnificent copy of the first volume includes a miniature showing the author presenting his book to the king in the presence of three companions. Edward spent the winter of 1470-1471 in exile in Flanders, when he was the guest of the great bibliophile Louis de Gruthuyse, first at The Hague and later in Bruges. The production of this volume may be a result of that visit. Later in the 1470s Edward himself embarked upon a sustained campaign of purchasing expensively illuminated manuscripts from the workshops of Bruges, laying the foundations of the English royal library which was eventually to pass into the keeping of the British Museum and Library.

175

Hours of William Lord Hastings

The Presentation; an English royal state barge

Flanders, probably Ghent, *c.*1480.
Latin; 165 x 125 mm, 300 fols.
Additional MS 54782, ff.125b–126

Coats of arms added in the borders of this beautiful book of hours identify it as the property of Edward IV's closest friend and supporter, William Lord Hastings. He was summarily executed in June 1483 by Edward's brother and successor, King Richard III, giving the manuscript a very precise date. Hastings followed the example of a number of his wealthy English contemporaries by ordering his books of personal devotion from the workshops in Flanders. Many of the pages in the manuscript are decorated with borders of naturalistic flower studies, a practice which became fashionable during the late 1470s in the circle of Duchess Mary of Burgundy, heiress of Charles the Bold and stepdaughter of Margaret of York.

d briefte et   fecque de ce luure. Car ie penffe
finguliere de   bien auoir proune on auoir en
ceste doleroufe   en woulente de celle chofe fare
vie linconfta   qui moult toft et legherement
ce et variable   peuft auoir efte empefchee por
te de fortune   aucune des caufes duant dict
la mutacion auffi de fa woulente   toutefuoies par maniere dun
et de fa penfee humaine font fe   petit prohefme Il me fault fare
caufee pourquoy ie nay point   aucunes declaracion neceffai
fait a ce commencement fe pro   res pour fentendement de ce luure

178

Statutes of the Order of the Golden Fleece

Maximilian of Austria as sovereign of the Order

Flanders, Bruges, *c*.1481.
French; 255 x 190 mm, 254 fols.
Harley MS 6199, f.73b

As consort of the reigning Duchess Mary, whom he married soon after she had succeeded her father in 1477, Maximilian of Austria became sovereign of the Order of the Golden Fleece, second only to the English Order of the Garter in age and prestige. His portrait and those of the two Burgundian dukes who preceded him are included in this richly illuminated copy of its statutes, made for Jean de Lannoy, Chancellor of the Order, soon after the chapter held on 6 May 1481. The chancellor was also Abbot of St Bertin and the arms of his community, as well as his personal arms, are included on the opening page.

176 (previous pages, left)

'Vita Christi; la Vengance de la Mort Jhesu Crist'

The Holy Trinity and the Annunciation

Flanders, Ghent, 1479.
French; 390 x 280 mm, 212 fols.
Royal MS 16 G. iii, f.18b

Painted with particular sensitivity in a style associated with manuscripts owned by Margaret of York, Duchess of Burgundy, and written out by the celebrated scribe David Aubert of Ghent, who also worked for her, this volume contains no marks of ownership but is dated 1479. It may have been a gift from Margaret to her brother the king when she made her first visit home to England from Burgundy in the summer of 1480. Edward's own collecting activities were probably influenced by his knowledge, through Margaret, of the superb library of the Dukes of Burgundy. Margaret herself enjoys lasting fame as the first patron of William Caxton, who introduced printing into England in 1476 after living for many years in Bruges.

177 (previous pages, right)

Valerius Maximus: 'Memorabilia'

The author at work

Flanders, Bruges, 1479.
French; 480 x 340 mm, 342 fols.
Royal MS 18 E. iii, f.24

This handsome manuscript is typical of the books commissioned by Edward IV from the workshops of Bruges in the late 1470s. It is one of several dated to 1479 and 1480, which seems to have been the most active period of his purchasing. The two volumes of this copy of the 'Memorabilia', in the French translation also owned by Philippe de Comines (172), contain nine large miniatures, all with elaborate borders incorporating Edward's arms and badges. In the lower border of this page his arms are enclosed within the ribbon of the Order of the Garter and flanked by two further shields representing his two sons, Edward Prince of Wales and Richard Duke of York, better known as the Princes in the Tower.

179

'Universal History from the Creation to 1340'

King David at the taking of Jerusalem

France, Bourges, 1480s.
French; 130 x 95mm, 100 fols.
Additional MS 26667, f.16b

The history of the world is here divided into six ages, the last of which begins with the death of Christ and ends with the Battle of Sluys in 1340. The seven miniatures are painted in the highly recognisable style associated with the name of Jean Colombe of Bourges, active during the last quarter of the 15th century. Colombe was a member of a family prominent in the arts for several generations. He pursued a very well patronised career as an illuminator and it is clear that he worked at the head of a substantial team which included his own son Philibert (died 1505). This miniature is very typical of the Colombe style, set in a wide and detailed landscape ad featuring an enormous crowd of 'extras' crammed into an impossibly small area.

180 (opposite)

William of Tyre: 'History of the Crusades'

The Emperor Heraclius carrying the True Cross

Flanders, Bruges, *c.*1479–1480.
French; 465 x 340 mm, 495 fols.
Royal MS 15 E. i, f.16

William of Tyre wrote his 'History of the Crusades' in the 12th century. Born in 1130, he became Patriarch of Tyre in 1167 and died in 1190. In the 54 illustrations which punctuate the text of this copy, events in the Near East are shown in the dress and settings of late 15th-century Flanders. The arms and devices of Edward IV appear amongst the marginal decoration, confirming that this was one of the works which he ordered for the English royal library.

181 (above)

Huth Hours

The annunciation to the shepherds

North-eastern France, Valenciennes, late 1480s.
Latin; 150 x 115 mm, 252 fols.
Additional MS 38126, ff.79b–80

This book of hours is one of the most richly decorated devotional books from the workshop associated with Simon Marmion (died 1489). Earlier in his career Marmion was responsible for the illumination of a number of grand secular volumes, including work carried out for Margaret of York, but in later years he is particularly associated with the production of books of hours of quite exceptional delicacy. In this example many of the pages are surrounded by borders scattered with individual flower heads so finely painted that they appear to have been blown onto the vellum surface.

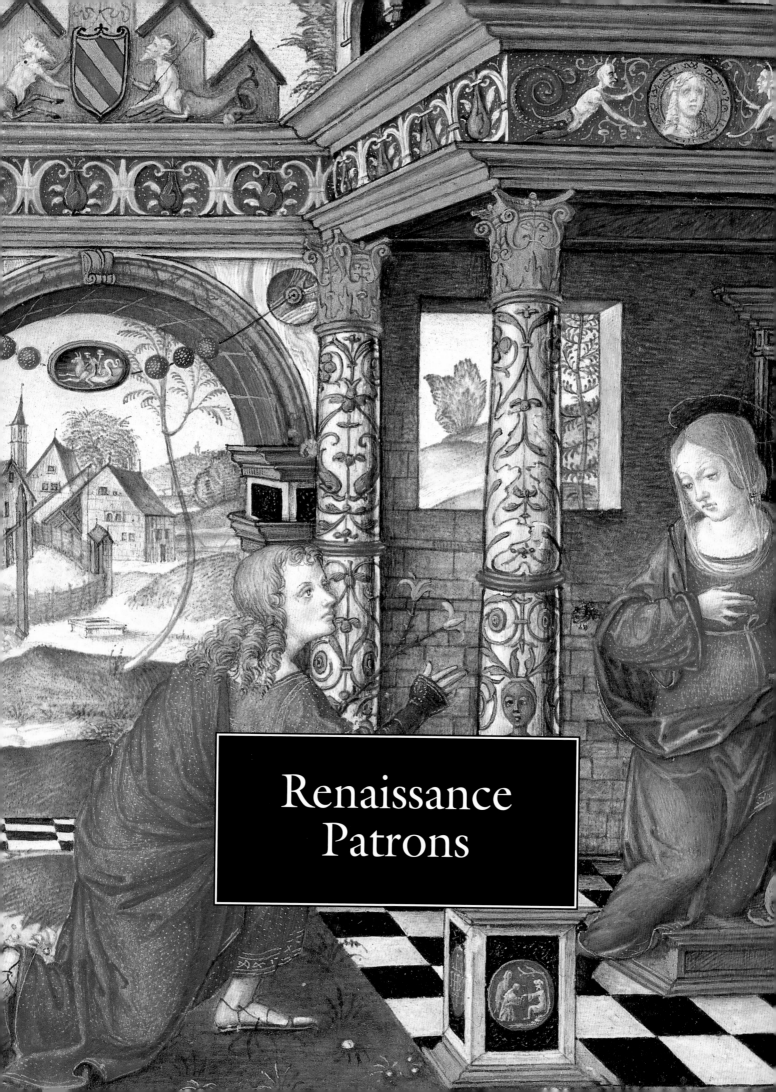

Renaissance
Patrons

During the last years of the 15th century the boundaries of the known world were dramatically extended as European explorers sought a sea route to the Indies, hitherto accessible only by land from the eastern end of the Mediterranean. Portuguese navigators had investigated the Atlantic seaboard of Africa and in 1488 Bartolomeu Dias for the first time rounded the Cape of Good Hope. The easterly sea route to the Indian sub-continent was finally established by Vasco da Gama in a voyage that lasted from July 1497 until September 1499. Meanwhile, two Italian-born seafarers, seeking a westerly route, established the presence of the Americas. Christopher Columbus, backed by Ferdinand and Isabella of Spain, discovered the West Indies in 1492 and John Cabot, sailing out of Bristol under the protection of Henry VII of England, made his landfall in Newfoundland in 1497. During the 16th century the politics of Europe increasingly extended into the New World.

In Europe itself dynastic links forged by Ferdinand and Isabella resulted in the early 16th century in an unprecedented alliance between Spain, the Burgundian Netherlands and the Germanic lands of the Holy Roman Empire. Spain itself had been united by the marriage in 1469 of Isabella of Castile and Ferdinand of Aragon. In 1492 they conquered Granada, driving the Moors from southern Spain. In 1497 two of their children, the Infante John of Asturias and the Infanta Joanna (afterwards nicknamed 'the Mad'), were married to the son and daughter of Maximilian of Austria, King of the Romans and afterwards Holy Roman Emperor, and Duchess Mary of Burgundy, heiress of Charles the Bold (191). In due course Joanna's son, Charles, found himself heir to Spain through his mother, to the Burgundian Netherlands through his father and, on the death in 1519 of his grandfather Maximilian, successful candidate for the imperial crown. Charles was at the same time closely linked to the Tudor King Henry VIII of England, whose first wife, Catherine of Aragon, was his aunt.

By the year 1500 the printed book was firmly established throughout Europe and had taken over much of the lower end of the general market formerly supplied by scribes and illuminators. Paris, in particular, became noted for the production of books of hours, published in varying degrees of sophistication by a number of presses. These were often elaborately decorated with illustrations and borders of woodcuts, which might additionally be overpainted by hand. The press of Anthoine Vérard was particularly noted for editions of large-scale secular library books, often printed on vellum and embellished with miniatures which include work in the styles associated with the names of Maître François and Jacques de Besançon (172). His customers included not only the French king but also King Henry VII of England, established on the throne in 1485 after his victory over the last Yorkist king,

Detail from figure 200

Richard III, at Bosworth. Henry appears quite genuinely to have preferred French workmanship and to have purchased printed books from choice, though one or two very handsome Flemish manuscripts certainly belonged to him (189). Magnificently illuminated printed books were also prepared in Italy for contemporary bibliophiles.

In Italy the princes of both church and state created libraries that were outstanding both for the quality of their contents and for the quality of the workmanship lavished on the books (182–185). In appearance these are very different in script and in style of illumination from the products of the northern workshops in Flanders (173, 190). Some of the patrons employed their own scribes and illuminators, many of them identifiable by name. Others employed professional booksellers such as Vespasiano da Bisticci of Florence (died 1498) to commission books on their behalf. Vespasiano's clients included Federigo da Montefeltro, Duke of Urbino, reputed to have scorned the notion of including any printed book upon his shelves. A substantial part of his manuscript collection, said to have cost 30,000 ducats, is preserved in the library of the Vatican. Other major collectors were the Aragonese kings of Naples (182) and, outside Italy itself, King Matthias Corvinus of Hungary (died 1490), whose second wife was Beatrice, daughter of the king of Naples. Alongside the elegant products destined for library shelves, workshops of Italian illuminators continued to produce elaborate and costly books of hours for their aristocratic and wealthy customers (186, 197, 199, 200).

Politically the history of Italy was very much influenced by the activities of the kings of France for a period of some 50 years at the end of the 15th and early in the 16th centuries. Three successive French sovereigns invaded the Italian peninsula in pursuit of claims to its territories arising from past family connections. King Charles VIII (1483–1498) set out to conquer the kingdom of Naples on the strength of his descent from the house of Anjou. His cousin and successor, Louis XII (1498–1515), a member of the house of Orléans, pursued a claim to Milan on account of his descent from Giangaleazzo Visconti and his daughter Valentina. Francis I (1515–1547) began his reign with a decisive victory at Marignano over the Swiss troops who were defending the young Maximilian Sforza of Milan. Four years later, on the death of the Emperor Maximilian, he had hopes of attaining the imperial crown and, frustrated of this by the accession of Charles V, entered into an alliance with King Henry VIII of England amidst the legendary splendours of the Field of the Cloth of Gold in 1520. Francis's struggle against Charles V, whose borders marched with his to the south, the east and the north-east of his kingdom, was to continue for the remainder of his reign, punctuated by such memorable events as his defeat (and subsequent imprisonment) at Pavia in 1527 and his victory at Ceresole in 1544, which was followed by the treaties of Crespy (1544) and Ardres (1546).

First-hand experience of Italy's artistic heritage is discernible in work carried out for French patrons of the period (194, 205). Francis I was especially anxious to import the best of the Italian renaissance into France and two outstanding figures, Leonardo da Vinci and Benvenuto Cellini, were among those persuaded to spend time north of the Alps. Leonardo, who had spent a long period in the service of Duke Ludovico Sforza of Milan before he was overthrown by Louis XII in 1499 and who was again in Milan between 1506 and 1513, passed the last three years of his life at Amboise, supported by a pension from the French king. Cellini, who undertook work in precious metals for many of the rulers of Europe during a distinguished, if erratic, career, worked at the French court for a period of several years in the early 1540s. During Francis's time the art of illumination flourished in his circle, the artistic descendants of Fouquet and Bourdichon continuing to supply small and very rich books to their fashionable clients (204, 208).

Illuminators of the Ghent-Bruges school also continued to be well supplied with discerning clients. The ladies of the Burgundian ducal family long played a vital part in sustaining the luxury book trade. Edward IV's sister, Duchess Margaret, had been a substantial patron in her own right (170) and her stepdaughter, Charles the Bold's daughter and heiress Mary, gave her name to one of the outstanding book painters of the late 15th century. In 1506 the Emperor Maximilian's daughter, Margaret of Austria, widow of Duke Phillibert of Savoy, moved to the Netherlands as Regent for her infant nephew, the future Charles V. She seems to have brought with her not only the incomplete Hours of Bona Sforza (209) but probably also the celebrated 'Très Riches Heures' of John, Duke of Berry (now in the Musée Condé at Chantilly), which certainly influenced subsequent work in her adopted territory. She was to prove a valuable patron. Illuminators such as Simon Bening (203, 210) enjoyed an international reputation with associated commissions. Gerard Horenbout and his children apparently had little difficulty in finding themselves employment outside the Low Countries in the mid 1520s, at the court of Henry VIII of England (207), where Gerard's son Lucas played a seminal part in the development of the art of the portrait miniature.

It was in England soon afterwards that the Reformation manifested itself in a particularly visible form, when Henry VIII (died 1547) broke decisively with Rome over the question of his divorce from Catherine of Aragon. This in itself would ultimately have undermined the traditional market for fine devotional and liturgical books. The subsequent suppression of the English monasteries and the destruction of such a high proportion of what was preserved in their libraries and sacristies was a huge tragedy for all subsequent students of the medieval book.

182 (opposite)

Duns Scotus: 'Quaestiones on the Sentences of Peter Lombard'

The author at work

Italy, Naples, *c.*1480–1485.
Latin; 425 x 280 mm, 269 fols.
Additional MS 15273, f.8

The original owner of this manuscript was Ferdinand I of Naples, son of Alfonso V of Aragon (158), whose library was one of the finest in Europe. The book is a large one but, by comparison with the scripts associated with the professional Flemish scribes of the day working on a comparable scale (173, 190), its humanistic roman script, the work of Pietro Ippolito da Luni, is very delicate. The complex white vine scroll decoration of the borders, incorporating Ferdinand's arms and emblems, is typical of the time, but the cool colours of the author miniature strike a distinctive note. The illuminator is thought to have been Cola Rapicano.

183 (above)

Eusebius: 'Chronica'

Introductory miniature of St Jerome with his lion

Italy, Rome or Padua, *c.*1480–1490.
Latin; 330 x 230 mm, 150 fols.
Royal MS 14 C. iii, f.2

St Jerome translated the 'Chronica' into Latin from the original Greek of Eusebius, Bishop of Caesarea (active *c.*300–340). The work offers a comparative chronology of biblical, Roman and other events, listed by country. This splendid copy was made for Bernardo Bembo (1433–1519), a prominent politician in Venice who served as governor successively of Ravenna, Bergamo and Verona. He was the father of Pietro Bembo, the celebrated author and cardinal. The manuscript was written out for him by his close friend Bartolommeo Sanvito of Padua (184) and decorated probably by Gaspare da Padova, at one time a member of the household of Cardinal Francesco Gonzaga (died 1483). The illuminator's style is much indebted to the work of Andrea Mantegna, who was court painter to the Gonzaga of Mantua from 1460.

P·VIRGILII MARO
NIS AENEIDOS
LIB·II·
ONTICVE
RE OMNES
INTEN
TIQ·ORA
TENEBANT·

I nde toro pater æneas sic orsus ab alto.
I nfandum regina iubes renouare dolorem.
T roianas ut opes & lamentabile regnum
E ruerint danai: quæq; ipse miserrima uidi:

184 (opposite)

Virgil: 'Eclogues, Georgics and Aeneid'

The wooden horse entering the gates of Troy; Anchises carried from the city by Aeneas

Italy, Rome, *c.*1490.
Latin; 285 x 180 mm, 244 fols.
King's MS 24, f.73b

Bartolomeo Sanvito (183) was responsible for the script in this copy of the works of Virgil and it is possible that he provided at least some of the decoration. A native of Padua, born in 1435 and still alive in 1518, he was a man of property, a canon of Monselice, a connoisseur and a collector, as well as one of the most distinguished scribes of the age. About 40 surviving books can be attributed to his hand. He moved to Rome in the mid 1460s and worked for a clientele that included Pope Sixtus IV and Cardinal Francesco Gonzaga. This manuscript was apparently made for Lodovico Agnelli, apostolic protonotary, who was associated with both men, at some time before he became Archbishop of Cosenza in 1497.

185 (above)

Petrarch: 'Poems'

Petrarch and Laura

Italy, Milan, end of the 15th century.
Italian; 200 x 125 mm, 88 fols.
Additional MS 38125, f.58

In 1327 the great humanist poet Francesco Petrarca (1304–1374) met a young married woman in Avignon and promptly fell in love with her. Her name was Laura and he was to remain devoted to her for the remainder of his life, though she in fact died in the Black Death in 1348. His celebrated 'Trionfi' record a vision which he experienced in his sleep on one of the anniversaries of their meeting. In this miniature, which accompanies the 'Trionfo della Morte', he is seen, crowned with laurel, conversing with his dead love. The manuscript which also contains some of Petrarch's 'Sonetti' and 'Canzoni', was apparently made in Milan for a member of the Romei family of Ferrara and is illustrated in a style closely related to that of Giovan Pietro Birago, court painter to the Sforza dukes during the 1490s.

186

Book of Hours

The birth of the Virgin Mary

Italy, Milan, end of the 15th century.
Latin; 95 x 75 mm, 158 fols.
Additional MS 35316, ff.81b–82

Extremely small in scale, this book of hours contains six miniatures in the style of the Milanese court painter Giovan Pietro Birago, best known for his work in the original portion of the Hours of Bona Sforza (209). Birago signed work carried out for Brescia cathedral in the early 1470s. In Milan he was clearly supported by a substantial workshop. His work has a rich and jewel-like quality. He survived the French invasion of Milan in 1499 and is last heard of in a letter written in April 1513.

187

Book of Hours

The Annunciation to the shepherds

France, Tours, *c*.1490.
Latin; 145 x 95 mm, 123 fols.
Harley MS 2877, f.51b

Jean Bourdichon (died 1521) succeeded Fouquet (163) as court painter to the kings of France, serving in turn Louis XI, Charles VIII, Louis XII and Francis I. Little of his large-scale work has survived but his hand appears in many illuminated manuscripts, often alongside those of his numerous pupils and assistants. His undoubted masterpiece is a magnificent book of hours made for Louis XII's queen, Anne of Brittany, for which payment was authorised in 1508. It includes more than 300 marginal illustrations of flowers and plants, all identified in Latin and in French. In this smaller and less elaborate book Bourdichon's preoccupation with depicting visible sources of light is beautifully demonstrated in his miniature of the shepherds.

188

Book of Hours

The Annunciation to the shepherds

France, Tours, end of the 15th century.
Latin; 190 x 125 mm, 96 fols.
Additional MS 11865, f.32b

One of Bourdichon's contemporaries painted this version of the Annunciation to the shepherds, in sharp contrast to the sophisticated work of the established court painter. Although these figures are much livelier and more dramatic than those by Bourdichon (187), the picture as a whole lacks his depth and intensity. Both artists have however addressed the problem of integrating the entire surface of the vellum page, Bourdichon by presenting his subject as a small panel painting, framed and hung against a marble surface, this anonymous painter by floating the introductory lines of accompanying text on a scroll apparently suspended above the picture plane.

189 (opposite)

Poems of Charles of Orléans and other works

A lover addressing three ladies

Flanders, Bruges, *c*.1490–1500.
French; 375 x 260 mm, 248 fols.
Royal MS 16 F. ii, f.188

This manuscript was begun for Edward IV of England but left unfinished at his death in 1483. It was taken up again and completed for Henry VII, whose arms, impaled with those of his queen, Elizabeth of York, appear in the lower margin here flanked by the red and white roses that symbolise the houses of Lancaster and York. This is one of several miniatures commissioned for the book from the Master of the Prayerbooks of *c*.1500 (190), probably by Henry's librarian, Quintin Poulet of Lille. He was himself a professional scribe and illuminator trained in Flanders and probably knew the artist personally. It introduces one of the subsidiary works in the manuscript, 'Les demandes damours', and demonstrates the illuminator's love of painting fine fabrics and fashionable costumes.

190 (above)

Guillaume de Lorris and Jean de Meun: 'Roman de la Rose'

Primitive people in an idyllic past

Flanders, Bruges, *c*.1490–1500.
French; 395 x 290 mm, 186 fols.
Harley MS 4425, f.76b (detail)

The 'Roman de la Rose' is an allegorical poem of chivalric love, composed in the 13th century, which enjoyed an enormous popularity for the remainder of the Middle Ages. This unusual scene, showing the idyllic life of the ancient peoples who amassed no worldly goods and owed fealty to neither kings nor princes, comes from the finest of the many surviving illustrated copies, made at the end of the 15th century for Engelbert, Count of Nassau (died 1504), prominent member of the Burgundian ducal court. The anonymous illuminator is known as the Master of the Prayerbooks of *c*.1500, because most of the manuscripts from his workshop are books of hours. He was, however, responsible for a number of very grand secular manuscripts such as this, offering scope for a more imaginative approach to illustration (189).

191 (opposite)

Breviary of Isabella of Castile

The Entry into Jerusalem

Flanders, Bruges, before 1497.
Latin; 230 x 160 mm, 523 fols.
Additional MS 18851, f.96

Today best remembered as the patrons of Columbus's expedition to discover the New World, Queen Isabella of Castile and Leon (died 1504) and her husband, King Ferdinand of Aragon (died 1516), unified Spain under their joint rule and achieved the final expulsion of the Moors from Granada in 1492. This magnificent breviary was presented to her in 1497 by her ambassador Francisco de Rojas, to mark the marriages of two of her children to the son and daughter of Duchess Mary of Burgundy and Maximilian of Austria, King of the Romans. Its main miniatures are the most important works of an anonymous illuminator, known from one of his manuscripts as the Master of the Dresden Prayerbook.

192 (above)

Pierre Louis de Valtan: 'Commentary on the Apostles' Creed'

The author presenting his work to Charles VIII; St Peter

France, probably Tours or Bourges, before 1498.
Latin; 225 x 155 mm, 25 fols.
Additional MS 35320, ff.2b–3

King Charles VIII of France, who died in 1498, is shown here receiving this copy of the book from the hands of its author. The features of the author were added to the miniature by a specialist portrait painter and must be true to life. The miniatures of the 12 apostles, of which St Peter is the first, are attributable to a contemporary of Bourdichon (187), a brilliant master of the art of illumination recently identified with Jean Poyet, whose career is documented during the last years of the 15th century. His work was extravagantly admired during his lifetime and more and more manuscripts are now being associated with his name.

217

193 (opposite)

Book of Hours

The Virgin and Child with Angels

Flanders, Bruges or Ghent, *c*.1500.
Latin; 240 x 150 mm, 237 fols.
Additional MS 35313, f.46

The artist chiefly responsible for this very grand book of hours has been called the Master of James IV of Scotland because he also painted the miniatures in a book of hours made to mark the marriage of the Scottish king to Margaret, elder daughter of King Henry VII of England, in 1503. Their book is now in the Österreichische Nationalbibliothek in Vienna. Several further works, including parts of the Breviary of Isabella of Castile (191), can be attributed to him, making his one of the most successful workshops of the period. It is now widely held that he was in fact Gerard Horenbout, a native of Ghent, where he joined the appropriate guild in 1487. Horenbout was appointed court painter to Margaret of Austria, Regent of the Netherlands, in 1515 and is associated with the Flemish miniatures added for her to the Hours of Bona Sforza (209).

194 (above)

Pierre Sala: 'Emblesmes et Devises d'Amour'

Portrait of the author

France, Paris, *c*.1500.
French and Spanish; 130 x 100 mm, 21 fols.
Stowe MS 955, ff.16b–17

Pierre Sala, a native of Lyons, entered the service of the kings of France about 1480. He held a variety of positions and even in retirement retained the royal favour, being accorded the honour of a visit at his home by Francis I in 1522. This little book of illustrated verse, one of the most personal manuscripts in the Library's collections, was made to his order about 1500 as a gift for his ladylove, Marguerite Bullioud. The couple had apparently known each other in childhood and, each having meanwhile married and been widowed elsewhere, they were finally united about 1515–1519. Most of the book's miniatures are by a fashionable Parisian artist known as the Master of the 'Chronique scandaleuse' but this portrait of the author is attributable to Jean Perréal, a court painter celebrated for his skill in painting likenesses and a personal friend of Sala himself.

195

Book of Hours

The Seven Sorrows of the Virgin

Flanders, Bruges, *c*.1500.
Latin; 160 x 105 mm, 89 fols.
Additional MS 35314, f.72b

In this moving image the Seven Sorrows of the Virgin, seven episodes from the life of Christ are delicately painted in grisaille in roundels directed into the figure of Christ's mother along the blades of seven swords. In complete contrast to the starkness of the miniature, the border is filled not with the naturalistic flowers so fashionable in Flemish manuscripts of the time (181) but with splendid jewellery, the gold, enamel and gemstones of the individual ornaments painted so realistically that they appear detached from the surface of the page. It seems that manuscript illuminators quite often provided designs for jewellery and perhaps this painter was among their number.

196

Hours of Jean Lallemant the Elder

The raising of Lazarus

France, probably Bourges, *c*.1498.
Latin; 205 x 130 mm, 41 fols.
Additional MS 39641, f.19b

The Lallemant family were leading citizens of Bourges during the late 15th and early 16th centuries. They were also substantial patrons of the arts, commissioning a number of outstanding devotional books from the best artists of the day. This book of hours, which is unfortunately fragmentary, contains miniatures attributable to Jean Poyet (192) and displaying all the finest characteristics of his style. The rich, bright colours, lavishly highlighted with gold, the distinctive faces, and the convincing treatment of space and of light, all bear a family resemblance to the work of Poyet's contemporary, Jean Bourdichon (187) while remaining quite distinct from it. Both are ultimately dependent upon Fouquet (163). The Lallemant arms appear in the lower margin of the miniature.

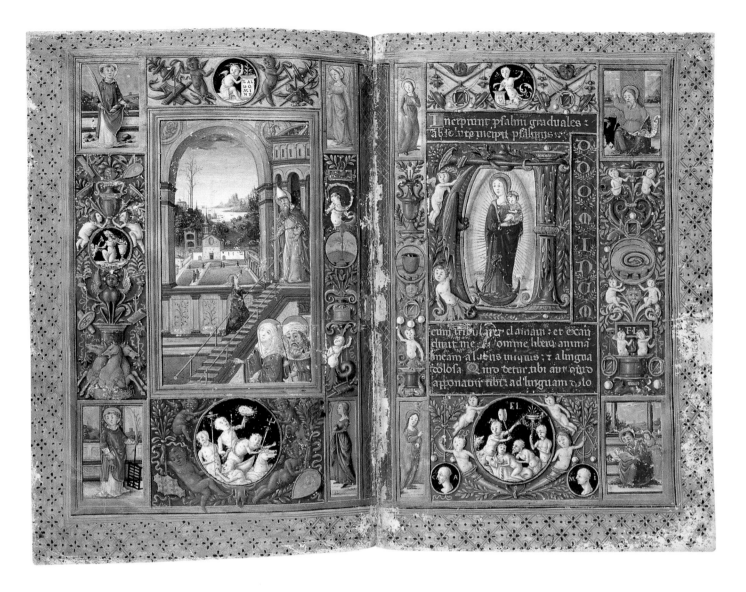

197

Hours of Laudomia de' Medici

The entry of the Virgin Mary into the Temple at Jerusalem

Italy, Florence, *c.*1502.
Latin; 180 x 120 mm, 131 fols.
Yates Thompson MS 30, ff.117b–118

Laudomia de' Medici, daughter of a cousin of Lorenzo 'the Magnificent', was married in 1502 to Francesco Salviati. This elaborately decorated book of hours was probably made to mark the occasion. It was ordered from the leading Florentine illuminators of the day, its 15 miniatures and their borders displaying work by Attavante degli Attavanti (1452–*c.*1517) and Giovanni Boccardi (1460–1529). These two pages introduce the gradual psalms with an image of the young Virgin Mary climbing the steps into the temple, where traditionally she was educated. In the accompanying decoration, antique and contemporary motifs are mingled in a bewildering display of colours and details.

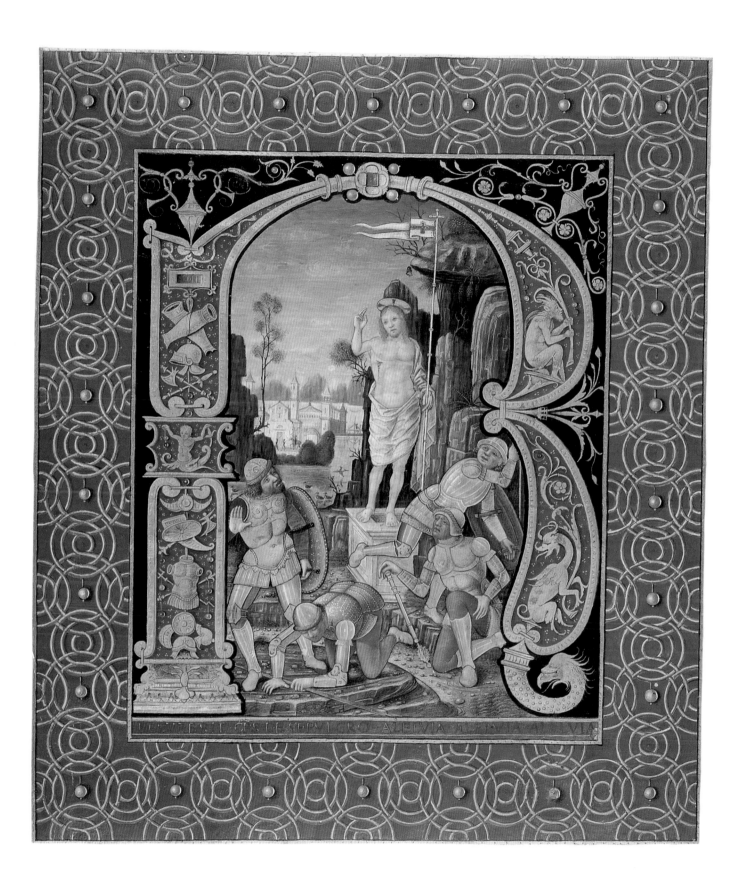

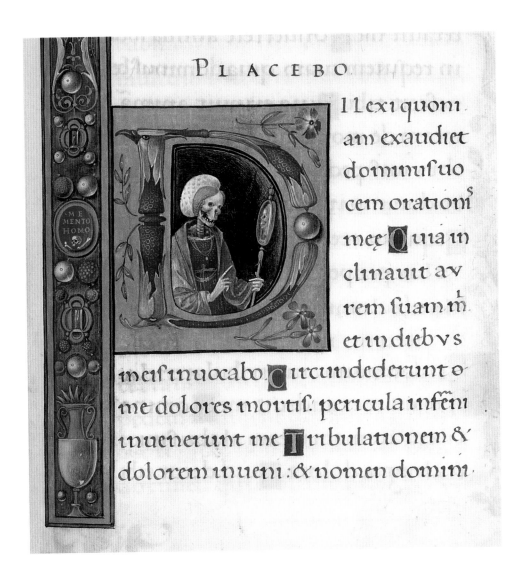

198 (opposite)

Cutting from a Choirbook

The Resurrection

Italy, probably Milan, *c*.1500.
Latin; 305 x 265 mm, detached cutting.
Additional MS 35254 D

The source of this cutting must have been a choirbook of
exceptional size and grandeur. Its pictorial style is clearly
influenced by that of contemporary painters working on a
much larger scale, such as Andrea Mantegna (1431–1506),
whose principal patrons were the Gonzaga dukes of Mantua,
and the supreme all-round genius Leonardo da Vinci
(1452–1519). Famed as a sculptor, an architect and an
engineer as well as for his graphic work, Leonardo entered
the service of the Sforza dukes of Milan during the 1480s.
The antique motifs in the frame of the initial letter R are very
characteristic of the period.

199 (above)

Hours of Dionora of Urbino

*'Memento mori': death gazing upon her reflection
in a looking glass*

Italy, probably Ferrara, *c*.1509–1520.
Latin; 210 x 140 mm, 219 fols.
Yates Thompson MS 7, f.174 (detail)

The decoration of this book, which was written out by the
scribe Matteo Contugi of Volterra, is confined to a series of
29 historiated or decorated initials with associated borders.
The original owner was Dionora, Duchess of Urbino (died
1543), born a member of the Gonzaga family, and married to
Francesco Maria della Rovere, nephew of Pope Julius II, to
whom the dukedom was bequeathed in 1508 by Guidobaldo
da Montefeltro. Although by comparison with illumination in
some of the other contemporary Italian books (197) the work
here appears simple; it is attributable to the school of Ferrara
and in particular to Matteo da Milano, who was working for
Duke Ercole I in 1502 (200).

200 (opposite)

Hours of Bonaparte Ghislieri

The Annunciation

Italy, Bologna, *c*.1500.
Latin; 205 x 150 mm, 136 fols.
Yates Thompson MS 29, f.74b

A reference in one of its prayers dates the execution of this book to the time of Pope Alexander VI (1492–1503) and a coat of arms which appears several times identifies the original owner as a member of the Ghislieri family of Bologna. The initials BP and GI suggest that he was probably Bonaparte Ghislieri, who served the city as a senator from 1523 until his death in 1541, though the manuscript may have been ordered by his father, Virgilio. Three major artists contributed to the book's decoration. This page is by Matteo da Milano, who was working for Duke Ercole I of Ferrara by 1502. Other miniatures are signed by Amico Aspertini (1475–1552) and Petro Vannucci, known as Perugino (1446–1524), both of whom are better known for work on a much larger scale.

201 (above)

'Disputacion de la Felicite Humaine'

Personification of Virtue

France, Paris, early 16th century.
French; 215 x 150 mm, 59 fols.
Cotton MS Caligula A. v, f.37

This little manuscript is neither elegantly written nor richly decorated, but its few miniatures appear to be attributable to Jean Pichore. Clearly documented as working in Paris between 1502 and 1520, Pichore was patronised by several members of the royal house, notably Louise of Savoy, the bibliophile mother of King Francis I. He also worked for Cardinal Georges d'Amboise, archbishop of Rouen, with whom the style that he represents is particularly associated. The cardinal built up a comprehensive library at his castle of Gaillon, many of the most richly illuminated books in which had been made to his personal order.

202

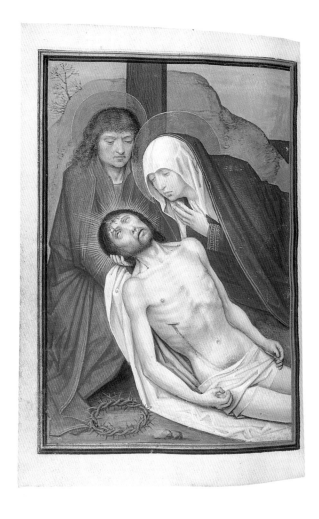

203

Pageants for the Marriage of Mary Tudor to Louis XII of France

The Three Graces with the lilies of France and the roses of England

France, Paris, 1514.
French; 270 x 170 mm, 15 fols.
Cotton MS Vespasian B. ii, f.6

In 1514, Mary, the 18-year-old younger sister of King Henry VIII of England, was dispatched to France as the unwilling bride of the ageing French King Louis XII. The match was a political one. As was the custom on such occasions, her state entry into Paris, as its future queen, was marked by a series of pageants along the route, each offering some symbolical comment on the event. The text accompanying each pageant, with a record of its appearance, is collected into this handsome souvenir volume which may have been intended for Mary herself. The marriage lasted only a few months. In 1515 Louis died and was succeeded by Francis I. Mary subsequently married one of her brother's oldest friends, Charles Brandon, Duke of Suffolk, and was the grandmother of the unhappy Lady Jane Grey.

Prayerbook of the Abbess of Messines

Pietà

Flanders, Bruges, 1516 or later.
Latin; 150 x 105 mm, 220 fols.
Egerton MS 2125, f.154b

The most successful member of the second generation of artists of the Ghent-Bruges school was Simon Bening, born in Ghent about 1483, whose career extended into the second half of the 16th century. This masterly painting of the Virgin grieving over the body of the dead Christ is attributable to him. It is among the miniatures in a book made probably for Joanna of Ghistelles, who was nominated abbess of Messines, near Ypres, in 1516 at the age of 17. The manuscript includes ceremonies peculiar to the abbey and the connection with Joanna is suggested by the presence of a rhymed office for the very unusual St Godelieva, patron of Ghistelles.

204

Book of Hours

David and Bathsheba

France, Tours, *c*.1515–1520.
Latin; 160 x 90 mm, 117 fols.
Additional MS 35315, f.52

Small-scale books of hours, illuminated with great richness, enjoyed a renewed popularity at the court of Francis I of France. This particular example has several unusual features, including its elongated format and the beautiful italic script, more usually associated with works of humanist scholarship than with books of devotion. The miniature, positioned within an architectural framework which looks back to Italian work, places the story of David's infatuation with Bathsheba firmly in a contemporary context. Its anonymous artist, a leading illuminator of the day who shared the illustration of this manuscript with Jean Poyet (192), is known as the Master of Claude of France in honour of Francis I's first wife, the daughter of Louis XII and Anne of Brittany.

205

François du Moulin and Albert Pigghe: 'Les Commentaires de la Guerre Gallique'

The Swiss dancing as their villages burn

France, Paris or Blois, 1519.
French; 250 x 125 mm, 76 fols.
Harley MS 6205, f.9b

The Harley 'Commentaires' is the first of a series of three volumes made to flatter the imperial ambitions of Francis I. Following very roughly the sequence of the first three books of Caesar's 'Gallic Wars', the text takes the form of conversations between Francis and Julius Caesar on their common experiences as conquerors of the Swiss, whom Francis had defeated at Marignano in 1515, and on the responsibilities of being emperor. The author, the Franciscan François du Moulin, had long been associated with the royal family and in particular with Francis's mother, Louise of Savoy, who may well have been the inspiration behind this project. The miniatures were painted by Godefroy le Batave, a Dutch artist trained in Antwerp and working in a self-consciously Antique style.

227

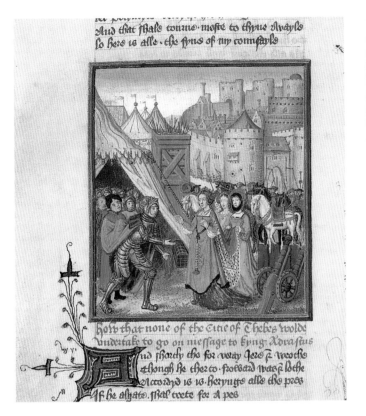

206 (opposite)

Polyphonic Music for Henry VIII

Symbols of the royal house of Tudor

Flanders, possibly Bruges, *c.*1516.
Latin; 495 x 345 mm, 17 fols.
Royal MS 11 E. xi, f.2

This magnificent composition, incorporating a whole range of the devices used symbolically by the early Tudors, introduces a volume of polyphonic music presented to King Henry VIII in or about 1516. Its verses are set to music overleaf. Henry shared many of the devices first used by his father and stylistically the page is very close to work done for Henry VII (189) and seems almost old-fashioned in the context of the younger man's reign. Circumstantial evidence as well as some of the detail of the miniature does however confirm the date. The pomegranate bush beneath the arms of Castile and Leon (right) stands for Catherine of Aragon, whom Henry had married soon after his accession in 1509. The daisy and the marigold at the foot of the rose tree stand for his two sisters, Margaret of Scotland (193) and Mary of France (202).

207 (above)

John Lydgate: 'The Siege of Thebes', and other works

(left) Jocasta's embassy to Adrastus;
(right) St Michael driving out Lucifer and his angels.

England, by a Flemish artist *c.*1525, in a manuscript written *c.*1465.
English; 395 x 280 mm, 212 fols.
Royal MS 18 D. ii, ff.158b, 161b (details)

Sir William Herbert and his wife, Anne Devereux, apparently ordered this volume of Lydgate's poetry as a gift for Edward IV about 1465. It remained unfinished when Herbert was executed after the Battle of Edgecote in 1469 and these two miniatures form part of a series of 17 subjects supplied during the mid 1520s to fill the gaps. They are clearly by Flemish rather than English hands and the St Michael is very close in style to the Horenbout additions in the Hours of Bona Sforza (209). Gerard Horenbout and his two children, Lucas and Susanna, did in fact migrate to England and into the service of Henry VIII at this time. Lucas was particularly successful and was responsible for introducing the art of portrait minia-ture painting to the English court. Susanna's work has never been identified though it was admired by Dürer when she was only 18 years old. It is tempting to attribute the Jocasta to her hand.

208

Book of Hours

David penitent; David making sacrifice

France, perhaps Paris, *c*.1525–1530.
Latin; 140 x 86 mm, 124 fols.
Additional MS 35318, ff.69b–70

The Master of Claude of France (204) was succeeded as main
supplier of richly decorated small books of hours to the court of
France by a group of illuminators working in a much more manner-
istic vein, though in many respects their work is indebted to that of
the earlier artist. The manuscripts are written out in fashionable
roman scripts and have often been related to the printed hours of
the Parisian Geofroy Tory. A knowledge of the work of Dürer and
of drawings, prints and paintings by the Antwerp Mannerists is also
quite clearly apparent. These miniaturists are most clearly
characterised by their choice of brilliant and unnatural colours.

209

Hours of Bona Sforza

Christ nailed to the cross

Flanders, Ghent, *c.*1517–1521.
Latin; 130 x 95 mm, 348 fols.
Additional MS 34294, f.12b

This is one of the series of miniatures added to the Hours of
Bona Sforza after it had passed into the hands of Margaret of
Austria, Regent of the Netherlands, at the beginning of the
16th century. The body of the book had been illuminated
around 1490 for the Duchess of Milan by Giovan Pietro
Birago (186) but a number of pages were lacking. Margaret
commissioned her own court painter, Gerard Horenbout, to
supply replacements. Although both in style and in concept
Horenbout's work is very different from that of Birago, the
Flemish master seems to have gone to great lengths in his
choice of pigments and in his treatment of the subsidiary
decoration, such as the putti on this page, to ensure that his
additions should blend in with the original work in the book.

210

Book of Hours

Calendar scene for October

Flanders, Bruges, *c.*1530.
Latin; 115 x 80 mm, 30 fols.
Additional MS 24098, f. 27b

This wonderfully detailed miniature celebrating the vintage is
one of a series of calendar illustrations attributable to Simon
Bening (203) at the height of his powers. The book of hours
to which they belong is now fragmentary and offers no signs
of origins or ownership. It has however become extremely
famous because it includes marginal scenes of contemporary
sports and pastimes, one of which bears a distinct resemblance
to the modern game of golf. The manuscript is usually known
for this reason as the 'Golf Book'. On this page the game
seen immediately below the main miniature is knucklebones,
played by children in scaled-down adult dress.

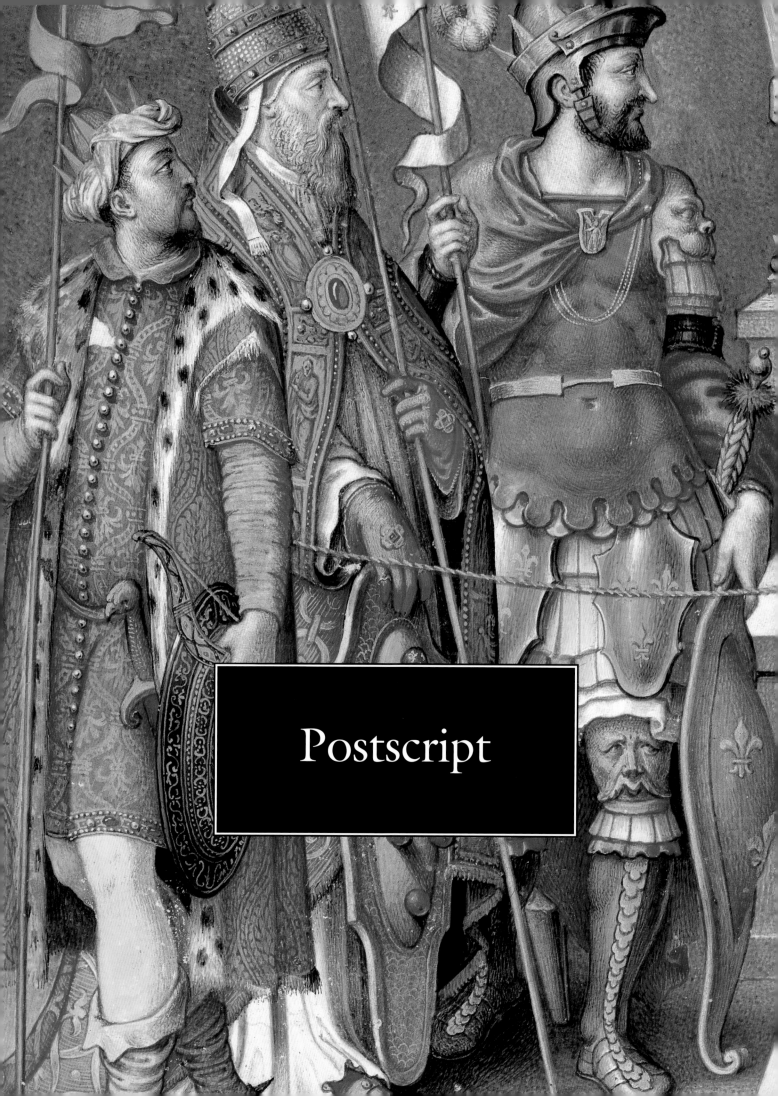

Postscript

The middle years of the 16th century marked a period of change and transition. The three long-established rulers who had dominated western Europe during the first half of the century were all replaced over a short space of time. Francis I of France and Henry VIII of England died within a few weeks of each other in 1547. The Emperor Charles V abdicated and retired to live out his days in monastic seclusion in Spain. Meanwhile every part of Europe was forced to make its own responses to the challenges of Reformation and Counter-Reformation, often resulting in the most bitter internal conflicts. At the same time international relationships were coloured by the rivalries and political manoeuvres spawned by an increasing awareness of the potential of the New World. Although very grand illuminated manuscripts continued for some time to find buyers among a small minority of wealthy bibliophiles in this very different world, the specialist craftsmen who produced them could no longer be regarded as practising a mainstream art form. The five very ostentatious manuscripts included in this last brief selection take the story into the mid 17th century and the reign of Louis XIV of France.

However, the illuminator's essentially medieval skills have never completely disappeared. In some specialised areas of production such as the decoration of grants of arms, patents of nobility or formal decorative genealogies the ability to paint and gild on vellum is required to this day. At the beginning of the 18th century a few professional calligraphers found themselves commissioned to copy early scripts and their accompanying decoration, in the interests of antiquarian studies. A century later, when more sophisticated methods of producing printed reproductions of early works of art were being introduced, but before the science of photography had been developed, there were openings for professional facsimilists, trained originally in the techniques required for the painting of portrait miniatures. These 'artists' were required to make faithful copies of medieval work to act as models for engravers and lithographers and some of them produced replicas that would not have disgraced the originals. A more general taste for the arts and crafts of the Middle Ages, fuelled by such popular sources as the novels of Sir Walter Scott (died 1832), even led to a widespread fashion for illumination as a drawing-room pursuit. Self-help manuals on 'missal painting' proliferated in Victorian times. In the sequel to *Little Women*, published in 1869, Louisa May Alcott's artistic heroine, Amy March, typically produced 'on leaves of vellum... beautifully illuminated different texts'.

Towards the end of the century William Morris (died 1896), author, painter, designer and antiquary, made a conscious effort to understand and replicate some of the techniques which he recognised in illuminated manuscripts. His lead was followed by the first generation of modern scribes and illuminators, whose pupils and successors are today to be found on both sides of the Atlantic.

Detail from figure 211

211 (above)

Triumphs of the Emperor Charles V

The Emperor enthroned among his enemies

Italy or Flanders, third quarter of the 16th century.
Spanish; 200 x 290 mm, 13 fols.
Additional MS 33733, f.5

This is one of a series of 12 brilliantly coloured miniatures
traditionally attributed to the Croatian illuminator Giorgio
Giulio Clovio (1498–1578), who worked in Rome under the
patronage of the hierarchy of the Catholic church. The book
was highly regarded by 19th-century English connoisseurs, to
whom his work represented the zenith of the illuminator's
art. It illustrates episodes from the career of the Emperor
Charles V, who abdicated in favour of his son in 1558, following a series of commemorative engravings published in
1556 by Hieronymus Cock. Modern opinion suggests that
Clovio is very unlikely to have painted these pages, which
were probably produced by a Flemish artist familiar with
Italian work. They do however seem to have been owned by
the Emperor's successor, Philip II, as they are said to have
come from the library of the Escorial Palace, Madrid.

212 (opposite)

Salomon Trismosin: 'Splendor Solis'

*Alchemists exploring the foundations of nature by
burrowing into the earth; Esther and Ahasuerus*

Germany, 1582.
German: 320 x 225 mm, 48 fols.
Harley MS 3469 f.13b

Illustrated with 22 magnificent full-page miniatures, the
Harley 'Splendor Solis' is one of the world's most famous
alchemical manuscripts. Its reputed author, thought to be a
fictitious figure, claims to have conquered old age and
rejuvenated himself by means of the philosopher's stone,
having learned the arts of alchemy through study in Germany
and Italy. The highly detailed paintings in the book look back
to Flemish and French work of the earlier part of the 16th
century. They offer, incidentally, a number of detailed scenes
of contemporary life alongside their more specifically alchemical content.

213 (above)

Psalter of the Earl of Arundel

Armorials of Henry Fitzalan, Earl of Arundel;
David penitent

England, London, with French decoration 1565.
Latin; 305 x 205 mm, 105 fols.
Royal MS 2 B. ix, ff.1b–2

Henry Fitzalan, Earl of Arundel (died 1580), was a leading
figure on the English political stage in the early years of the
reign of Elizabeth I. As leader of the Roman Catholic faction
he later became involved in the plots and intrigues surround-
ing Mary Queen of Scots. This manuscript was written out
for him by Petruccio Ubaldini, a Florentine calligrapher who
worked in England under his patronage. The decoration must
have been commissioned from a French illuminator, one of a
group undertaking work for the French royal family and their
court during the middle years of the 16th century.

214 (opposite, below)

Letters Patent of James I creating his heir Prince of Wales

James I presenting the document to his son

England, London, 1610.
Latin; 535 x 680 mm, single sheet
Additional MS 36932 (detail)

James I created his elder son Henry Prince of Wales and Earl of Chester on 4 June 1610. The young prince had already shown himself to be an artistic patron of decided tastes, employing Inigo Jones as his surveyor. His early death in 1612, aged only eighteen undoubtedly changed the course of English history. The charter is colourfully decorated and the faces were entrusted to a skilled professional, possibly the portrait miniaturist, Nicholas Hilliard (died 1619).

215 (above)

Book of Hours

The Flight into Egypt

France, Paris, *c.*1520 and mid 17th century.
Latin; 225 x 155 mm, 102 fols.
Additional MS 18853, ff.54b–55

Begun in the 1520s for Francis I of France but abandoned unfinished, this manuscript was completed more than a century later, apparently for Louis XIV, who succeeded to the throne in 1643 at the age of four. The text and the marginal decoration on the right-hand page belong to the earlier period, displaying Francis's salamander badge and his crowned initial F. The miniature dates from the middle of the 17th century. Luxury devotional manuscripts made an unexpected return to fashion in France during the reign of 'the Sun King'.

Suggestions for further reading

For the history of the British Library's collections *see* E. Miller, *That Noble Cabinet: a history of the British Museum* (André Deutsch, 1973) and N. Barker and the curatorial staff, *Treasures of the British Library* (British Library/Harry N. Abrams, 1988, re-issued in paperback, 1996).

Outline histories of the art of illumination are given by O. Pächt, *Book Illumination in the Middle Ages* (Harvey Miller, 1986, paperback 1994) and by C. de Hamel, *A History of Illuminated Manuscripts* (Phaidon, 1986, second edition 199?). For specialist terminology *see* M. P. Brown, *Understanding Illuminated Manuscripts: a guide to technical terms* (J. Paul Getty Museum and The British Library, 1994). The techniques practised by illuminators is discussed in J.J.G. Alexander, *Medieval Illuminators and their Methods of Work* (Yale University Press, 1992) and in C. de Hamel, *Scribes and Illuminators* (British Museum/University of Toronto Press, 1992).

The best comprehensive coverage of manuscripts of any single nationality is provided by the *Survey of Manuscripts Illuminated in the British Isles*, ed. J.J.G. Alexander, *Insular Manuscripts from the 6th to the 9th century* (1978); E. Temple, *Anglo-Saxon Manuscripts 900-1066* (1976); C.M. Kauffmann, *Romanesque Manuscripts 1066-1190* (1975); N.J. Morgan, *Early Gothic Manuscripts I 1190-1250* (1982) and *II 1250-1285* (1988); L.F. Sandler, *Gothic Manuscripts 1285-1385* (1986) and K.L. Scott, *Later Gothic Manuscripts 1390-1490* (1997). For more general information see M.J. Rickert, *Painting in Britain: the Middle Ages* (Pelican History of Art 1954, second ed. 1965); C. Nordenfalk, *Celtic and Anglo-Saxon Painting* (Braziller/Chatto and Windus 1977) and R. Marks and N. Morgan, *The Golden Age of English Manuscript Painting 1200-1500* (Braziller/Chatto and Windus 1981).

Specific groups of material from other centres are covered by F. Mütherich and J. Gaehde, *Carolingian Painting* (Braziller/Chatto and Windus 1977); W. Cahn, *Romanesque Bible Illumination* (Cornell University Press, 1982); H. Buchthal, *Miniature Painting in the Latin Kingdom of Jerusalem* (Clarendon Press, Oxford 1957); R. Branner, *Manuscript Painting in France during the Reign of St Louis* (University of California Press, 1977); F. Avril, *Manuscript Painting at the Court of France 1310-1380* (Braziller/Chatto and Windus, 1978); M. Thomas, *The Golden Age: manuscript painting at the time of Jean, Duc de Berry* (Braziller/Chatto and Windus, 1979); G. Dogaer, *Flemish Miniature Painting in the 15th and 16th centuries* (BM Israel BV 1976) and J.J.G. Alexander, *Italian Renaissance Illuminations* (Braziller/Chatto and Windus 1977).

In recent years a number of outstanding exhibition catalogues have been published, offering a wide range of information and reproductions in specific areas. Of particular note are: *Renaissance Painting in Manuscripts* (Hudson Hills Press/J. Paul Getty Museum, Malibu and British Library 1983); *The Golden Age of Dutch Manuscript Painting* (Rijksmuseum het Catharijne-convent, Utrecht and Pierpont Morgan Library, New York, 1989); *Les Manuscrits à Peintures en France 1440-1520*, ed. F. Avril and N. Reynaud (Bibliothèque nationale, Paris, 1993); *Painting and Illumination in Early Renaissance Florence 1300-1450* (Metropolitan Museum of Art, New York, 1994) and *The Painted Page: Italian Renaissance Book Illumination 1450-1550* (Prestel/Royal Academy of Arts, London and Pierpont Morgan Library, New York, 1994).

The British Library has published monographs on several individual items featured in this book: C. Donovan, *The de Brailes Hours* (1991); M. Evans, *The Sforza Hours* (1992); M. Davies, *The Gutenberg Bible* (1996); J. Backhouse, *The Luttrell Psalter* (1989), *The Bedford Hours* (1990), *The Isabella Breviary* (1993), *The Lindisfarne Gospels: a masterpiece of book painting* (1995) and *The Hastings Hours* (1996).

Index of manuscripts

Frontispiece

Jean de Courcy: 'Chemin de Vaillance'
Nature shows Vaillance to the author in
a dream

Flanders, Bruges, late 1470s
French; 470 x 345mm, 345 fols
Royal MS 14 E. ii, f.1

Half - titlepage

Brunetto Latini: 'Li livres dou tresors'
Falcons

North-east France, early 14th century
French; 315 x 225 mm, 162 fols
Yates Thompson MS 19, f.54 (detail)

Titlepage

Jean Cuvilier: 'Chronique de Bertrand du
Guesclin'

Coronation of the king and queen of Castile
France, probably Paris, about 1400
French; 305 x 225 mm, 289 fols
Yates Thompson MS 35, f.136 (detail)

Vignette on contents page
See figure 98, f.304 (detail)

Front of jacket
See figure 77 (detail)

Back of jacket
The marriage at Cana, *see* figure 133, f.276
(detail)

Front flap

Alani de Insulis: 'Summa de arte
praedicandi'

The sixth attitude of prayer
Swabia, Ottobeuren, second quarter
of the 13th century
Latin; 320 x 240 mm, 218 fols
Additional MS 19767, f.196b (detail)

Back flap

February, *see* figure 127, f.2 (detail)